FORAGING

FORAGING

13-Digit ISBN: 978-1-64643-339-1
10-Digit ISBN: 1-64643-339-4

This book may be ordered by mail from the publisher. Please include $5.99 for postage and handling. Please support your local bookseller first!

Books published by Cider Mill Press Book Publishers are available at special discounts for bulk purchases in the United States by corporations, institutions, and other organizations. For more information, please contact the publisher.

Cider Mill Press Book Publishers
"Where good books are ready for press"
501 Nelson Place
Nashville, TN 37214

Visit us online!
cidermillpress.com

Typography: Futura PT, URW DIN

Printed in China

Images used under official license from Shutterstock.com.

1 2 3 4 5 6 7 8 9 0
First Edition

FORAGING

AN ILLUSTRATED GUIDE TO
EDIBLE WILD PLANTS

DR. KIT CARLSON AND **AARON CARLSON**

CIDER MILL PRESS

BOOK PUBLISHERS

TABLE OF CONTENTS

INTRODUCTION

Throughout almost all human history, the ability to successfully find, harvest, and use food, fiber, and medicine from the environment was the difference between survival and death. Some anthropologists theorize that the human need to forage in complex and often treacherous environments is a primary evolutionary driver of encephalization (big brains) in the human species. Some even claim that the challenges of foraging are what made humans human. Thinking about our foraging human ancestors can help us improve all aspects of our modern-day foraging efforts. In this context, a successful forager does not just find and harvest a resource. A successful forager stays safe and injury-free so they can forage in the future, does not consume toxic plants or fungi, continues to learn about their environment to become an increasingly effective forager, and forages sustainably, ensuring that there will be more to gather in the future.

KNOW BEFORE YOU GO:
SAFETY

SAFE FORAGING RULES:

- Learn to identify the edible and poisonous plants and fungi in your foraging area.
- Do not harvest from contaminated water or land.
- Be aware of your surroundings.
- Do not rely on a common name when researching your plant.

1) LEARN TO IDENTIFY THE EDIBLE AND POISONOUS PLANTS AND FUNGI IN YOUR FORAGING AREA.

One of the most critical steps before beginning to forage for edible plants and fungi is learning to identify the poisonous species in your foraging area. Only a few species are lethal in tiny quantities, but they can be abundant in specific regions and seasons. Other species may not be deadly poisonous but can cause adverse effects on the human body, enough to keep you in bed for a few days or worse. Some toxic species look like edible species, and identification takes skill and experience. Sometimes identification may only be possible by examining microscopic features, such as fungal spores. There are tragic stories of foragers misidentifying a plant or mushroom and ending up in the hospital or even dying. You should not harvest and consume a specimen unless you are confident in the identification.

Time and practice are critical to learning how to identify forage plants and fungi. Before embarking on this endeavor, you should start with the basics. For example, you might read a botany textbook or take a botany class to help learn the technical terms and structures used to identify species. The glossary of terms provided in this book is a starting point, but you should use more than one reference book or field guide to confirm your identification. Many reference books become outdated over time or may include inaccurate information. It is best to cross-reference more than one source to help ensure a potential identification you make is correct. Participating in local groups of foragers or partnering with other plant enthusiasts is another good way to help you learn how to identify the edible and poisonous species in your area.

With the advent of artificial intelligence and machine-learning technologies, online identification tools are often used and have become increasingly accurate. Unfortunately, they are not 100% accurate. Please do not use these tools to confirm the identity of a forage specimen you or others will consume. That being said, they can point you in the right direction and be helpful tools when learning to identify new plants and fungi. An excellent example of this is iNaturalist.org. Users can upload a photo and get a list of suggested identifications on this website. Other users can validate or refute identifications to improve overall accuracy.

Becoming proficient in plant and fungi identification is a skill that takes many years to develop, and you will become discouraged and ultimately unsuccessful if you try to learn everything at once. Minute details may distinguish a poisonous species from a safe forage species, and those can take time, practice, and dedication to learn and remember. It is best practice to start slow and focus on learning just a few species each season. Start with your area's easy and common forage species that do not have poisonous look-alikes. Determine how to identify these species, the habitats they are found in, and what parts to harvest. This book includes a quick reference for each entry highlighting these key points.

2) DO NOT HARVEST FROM CONTAMINATED WATER OR LAND.

Many plants and fungi have a unique capacity to accumulate toxins from the water, air, and soil. Some plants are so effective at accumulating toxins that they are used to bioremediate contaminated environments. Heavy metal contamination is of particular concern. Aquatic plant species tend to bioaccumulate more heavy metals than other plants. Avoid foraging near roads, construction sites, old quarries, mines, or other industrial sites. Waterborne pathogens may also be present in aquatic plants. Avoid harvesting plants that are near runoff sites or agricultural land. Foraged edibles are safest when cooked.

3) BE AWARE OF YOUR SURROUNDINGS.

Whether foraging in an urban environment or somewhere remote, it is best practice to forage with a partner and let people know where you will be foraging—scope out your forage location before your forage day. In urban habitats, consider hazards like traffic, unsupervised pets, curious people, broken glass, and other sources of injury. In more remote environments, consider risks like cliffs or other places you could stumble, open water, wild animals, fallen tree hazards, brambles, and getting lost. Never risk your health and safety for a foraging opportunity. Informing others of your location, going with a partner, making a plan, staying focused, and preparing for the environment you will be foraging in will help keep your adventure safe and fun.

4) DO NOT RELY ON A COMMON NAME WHEN RESEARCHING YOUR PLANT.

Common names for plants and fungi can tell us something interesting or useful about the plant. For example, Milk Thistle is the common name for *Silybum marianum*, a widely used galactagogue—a substance that increases breast milk production in lactating people. Problems occur when there are numerous common names, regionally specific ones, or when multiple plants have the same common name. Sometimes a plant that is safe to forage and a toxic plant will have the same common name. Avoid these problems by learning and using the scientific names of plants and fungi. The scientific name includes the genus and the specific epithet. The genus includes all the species in the

group, and the specific epithet distinguishes between particular species. In the Milk Thistle example above, *Silybum* is the genus, and *marianum* is the specific epithet. Together,
Silybum marianum is the species. The species is written with the genus name capital-
ized and the specific epithet in lowercase. It should be italicized or underlined. Quality
reference guides will use the correct format; you should be wary of guides that do not use
scientific names or do not use the valid format for scientific names.

KNOW BEFORE YOU GO:
SUSTAINABLE AND ETHICAL FORAGING

SUSTAINABLE FORAGING RULES:

- Learn about the threatened and endangered species in your area.

- Do not forage in fragile or protected habitats.

- Only take what you need; never take all.

- Start with weeds and invasive species.

1) LEARN ABOUT THE THREATENED AND ENDANGERED SPECIES IN YOUR AREA.

In the United States, more than 1,400 species are federally listed as endangered or threatened. An endangered species is imminently in danger of extinction. In contrast, a threatened species is likely to become endangered in the foreseeable future, given its current population trend. Without the proper permits, it is illegal to harvest/possess/transport any species on this list. Most of us are familiar with some more "charismatic" endangered species, such as the California Condor and the Gray Wolf, but how many people have heard of Nevin's Barberry or the Furbish Lousewort? A recent survey (2018) by the Association of Zoos and Aquariums found

that the average American thinks there are about 100 species on the endangered list. A would-be forager must become familiar with the endangered species in their foraging area.

Individual states also designate protected species based on their population trends within the states' boundaries. In most cases, it is illegal to harvest and possess these species. Many of these species will not be on the federal list and therefore are only protected within the state(s) they are listed. For some species, it may be illegal to harvest in one state while perfectly legal in a neighboring state. It is often the case that state-listed species are at the very edge of their natural range in the state(s) in which they are listed. One example is the Round-leaved Sundew (*Drosera rotundifolia*). This small, carnivorous plant is quite common in the numerous bogs found in Minnesota and Wisconsin and is not listed in those states. However, it is listed as endangered in Iowa and Illinois due to the scarcity of suitable habitats. To avoid potential legal problems, become familiar with the protected species in the location(s) where you intend to forage. The U.S. Fish and Wildlife Service maintains a database of federally listed species on its website. Individual states catalog the state-listed species.

2) DO NOT FORAGE IN FRAGILE OR PROTECTED HABITATS.

Before foraging a particular area, you should become familiar with the various habitats and microhabitats present within it and the susceptibility of these habitats to human incursions. No habitat is entirely immune to human presence or disturbance. Just the act of walking through a particular area affects the natural environment. Your presence or voice alters some species' behavior, whether scaring them off or attracting them. And while this is generally considered harmless, with no long-term effects, a long-term sustained presence of humans can have detrimental effects on many species.

While the presence of a human may or may not have a long-term effect on the species in an area, exploring a site will have some effects, the severity of which will depend on the specific type of habitat. Each step you take tramples vegetation and compresses the soil. In most habitats, plants can withstand some trampling with no real long-term effects. Still, repetitive steps in the same spots will ultimately affect the plant species present and lead to the formation of a trail with compacted soil and minimal vegetation. Eventually, this can lead to an increase in erosion and overall degradation of the area. Some habitat types are more prone to step-induced destruction than others. Soils that are already hardened or covered by a thick layer of duff and with sparse vegetation will be able to withstand more foot traffic than soils that are light and thin or normally saturated with water, such as those found in various types of wetlands. Examples of other kinds of habitats that tend to be less resistant to human incursions are tidal mudflats, sand dunes, bogs, and alpine/tundra habitats.

Another potential impact of human incursion into a habitat is the introduction of non-native species. Humans are a vector for spreading these species, especially those that have evolved to have animal-assisted dispersal of seeds, such as those that readily stick to hair and fabrics. Unbeknownst to us, we commonly have a variety of seeds or other plant propagules attached to us, whether on our shoes, clothes, or hair. Foragers should be mindful of this and be vigilant about ridding themselves of any potential seeds or other plant propagules before entering and leaving a specific area.

3) ONLY TAKE WHAT YOU NEED; NEVER TAKE ALL.

Just like making a plan for your safety, you should make a plan to be sustainable and ethical about your foraging. Know what you intend to forage and how it will be harvested, processed, and used. Too often, foragers harvest first and think later, resulting in pointless waste and habitat destruction. Your forage plan should emphasize only taking what you will use and being very conservative in your harvest. Never take the first or only forage plant or fungus, and never harvest everything. A good general guideline is to gather only 10–20 percent of the forage-able plants or fungi at a particular location. Foraging can be done sustainably and thoughtfully, but it takes planning and eth-ical behaviors to prevent further damage to the environment.

4) START WITH WEEDS AND INVASIVE SPECIES.

Many species included in this book were selected because they are weedy and abundant or invasive. These are often good forage options because removing these through forage may reduce invasive plant populations and create more habitat for native species to flourish. The same foraging ethics should be employed even when foraging for weeds or invasive species. Invasive species foragers should pay close attention to where and how they dispose of any plant material that could establish new populations of an invasive species. Great care should be taken to prevent the spreading of seeds or vegetative propagules of invasive species to new locations.

KNOW BEFORE YOU GO:
SUGGESTED FORAGING TOOLS AND RESOURCES

- Mushroom knife
- Trowel
- Container(s)
- Field notebook
- Waders
- Reference guides
- Appropriate outerwear (location and season)
- Bug spray, mosquito net
- Map of your forage area
- Water

You do not need to purchase expensive or sophisticated gear to forage. Creativity and forethought can go a long way in making your forage experience safe, sustainable, fun, and productive. My grandma would tie a Cool-Whip container to her belt every time she took a walk or a bike ride in the summer in case she came across harvestable berries. This action cost her nothing and resulted in many delicious pies over the following year!

One thing you may want to invest in is a mushroom knife for harvesting and brushing the debris off mushrooms and other items. I prefer a knife that folds to one worn on a belt in a sheath, but that is a personal preference. A forage container is another must-have. You probably already have something you can use or

adapt to be an excellent forage container. Something wearable that allows you to keep your hands free is a good option, including smaller containers that protect fragile foods like mushrooms and berries. Make thoughtful choices about your outerwear and shoes. Expect brambles, bugs, uneven terrain, and variable weather conditions. Your clothes and footwear may get damaged or covered with seeds and other debris. Mosquitoes, horseflies, and wood ticks may also be encountered. Plan for how you will avoid them and check for ticks on yourself, your loved ones, and your pets when you return. Bring plenty of water for all participants.

HOW TO USE THIS GUIDE

This guide provides an overview of commonly encountered forage plants and fungi, including basic identification features, how and when to harvest, and some suggested uses. Each entry includes a "quick reference." Check out the quick reference to see the forage uses, season, parts, and particular concerns (such as poisonous look-alikes) for each entry.

Plants are organized alphabetically by genus, though the mushroom are all found at the end. Use the index to look up plants by common name or genus.

This guide is intended to be used in conjunction with additional field guides and training to confirm the identification of forage plants and fungi.

You should never consume or use a plant or fungus without 100% confidence in your ability to identify the plant or fungus. Forage at your own risk.

MAPLE

Acer spp.

PLANT: A genus of mostly deciduous shrubs and trees from 2.5–45 m in height. Shrubby species are often multi-trunked.

LEAVES: Leaves are opposite in arrangement, with most species having palmately lobed leaves, with anywhere from 3 to 13 lobes, depending on the species. Some species have either compound or unlobed leaves. Many species are noted for their brilliant fall color.

FLOWERS: Maples may be either monoecious or dioecious. Flowers are borne in few to many flowered clusters that are usually drooping to some degree. Flower clusters are axillary or terminal on twigs, sometimes both. They are five-parted, small, and somewhat inconspicuous, although some species have larger, showier flowers. Coloration ranges from yellowish to reddish. They mostly flower in early spring, usually slightly before or concurrently with leaf emergence.

FRUITS: Their distinctive fruits are called samaras and consist of a pair of nutlets, each enclosed in a papery shell with wing-like extensions. They are designed to spin as they are released and fall to the ground, leading to some commonly used nicknames such as "helicopters" and "whirlybirds."

ROOTS: Large root systems are formed, usually as wide as the tree's canopy. The trees produce a thick, dense mat of thick roots just below the soil surface.

DISTRIBUTION AND HABITAT

At least 25 species (not all native) can be found throughout North America, occupying many habitats. They are mostly shade-tolerant and are common components of many forest types in North America. They are also popular ornamental and landscaping trees, with many native and non-native species planted outside their native range and habitats.

FORAGING

The Indigenous peoples of several parts of North America have been gathering sap from Maple trees for millennia. In the simplest systems, the sap is collected by drilling a small hole (about 4 cm deep) into the tree just past the bark, inserting a spigot, and attaching a bucket. The most abundant sap flow occurs when nights are below freezing and the days are warm, typically in early spring. The tree size, species, and temperature conditions will heavily influence sap production, but a typical tree produces about 20 liters of sap in a year. Maple syrup is made from the sap by slowly boiling off the water. Tree sap contains about 2% sugar, and Maple syrup is about 66% sugar. "Sugar shack" refers to the cabins where larger-scale boiling facilities are housed to make Maple syrup. Maple sap collection is not limited to North America; for example, in North Korea, sap from the Painted Maple or Gorosoe (*Acer mono*) is collected in the spring. The Gorosoe Maple water is

believed to be very healthy and promotes the expulsion of toxins from the body. The seeds from Maple trees can also be harvested and are edible in any season, although spring seeds are the least bitter and best tasting.

QUICK REFERENCE:

USES: edible

FORAGE SEASON(S): spring, summer, fall, winter

FORAGE PART(S): seeds, sap

SPECIAL CONCERNS: none

YARROW
KNIGHT'S MILFOIL
STAUNCHWEED
WOUNDWORT
BAD MAN'S PLAYTHING

Achillea millefolium

PLANT: Herbaceous perennials up to 70 cm tall. Stems are erect and may be singular or branched, often densely covered with short hairs, although some may be nearly hairless.

LEAVES: Leaves are spirally arranged on the stem and are up to 20 cm long. The lobes are slender and pinnate, giving the leaf a lacy, fern-like appearance. The leaves are usually sparsely covered with short, soft hairs (pubescent).

FLOWERS: Flowers occur in flattened clusters of 10–100 at the tops of the stems. Flowers are of the composite type and are up to 8 mm wide. Each flower has 3–8 ray florets, which are usually white but may be pink or purplish, and 10–20 white or grayish disc florets.

FRUITS: Dry, one-seeded fruits. The seeds are elliptical to lanceolate in shape, with winged margins, and are 1–2 mm long.

ROOTS: Roots are fibrous and numerous. Underground stems (rhizomes) are found in the top 10 cm of the soil.

DISTRIBUTION AND HABITAT

Yarrow can be found throughout North America. They are found in various habitats, such as meadows, roadsides, woodlands, and waste places.

FORAGING

Yarrow is an important folk medicine used worldwide to treat many conditions, including skin ailments, high blood pressure, menstrual cramps, colds and flu, and much more. It is referred to as "the woman's herb" because it has been used to control heavy menstrual bleeding or prompt an absent menstrual cycle. Laboratory and clinical evidence support the efficacy of some folk and traditional uses of Yarrow. For example, phytochemical analysis has revealed compounds in Yarrow extracts that are antibacterial, antiviral, and anti-inflammatory. An alkaloid found in Yarrow, achilleine, increases the rate of blood clotting and speeds wound healing. Compounds extracted from Yarrow are used in several patented prescription medications to treat dermatoses, uterine fibroids, and chronic colitis. Despite the numerous potential medicinal applications of Yarrow, excessive consumption can cause digestive ailments, and topical applications can cause allergic reactions. Although this herb is powerful, therapeutic applications should be used with caution and under the direction of an expert herbalist or healer.

Yarrow flowers can produce a colorfast yellow to tan dye; including the leaves with your flowers in your dye bath will alter and mute the color. Flowers can be harvested throughout the flowering season and used fresh or stored for later use.

QUICK REFERENCE:

USES: medicinal, dye

FORAGE SEASON(S): spring, summer

FORAGE PART(S): roots, stems, leaves, flowers

SPECIAL CONCERNS: It contains thujone, a neurotoxin.

SWEET FLAG
SWAY
MUSKRAT ROOT

Acorus calamus, Acorus americanus

PLANT: Herbaceous perennials that resemble Cattails in overall appearance. The leaves and roots emit a pleasant fragrance when crushed.

LEAVES: The sword-shaped leaves are basal and mostly erect, up to 1.8 m long and 2 cm wide, with overlapping, sheathing bases, like an iris. They are usually a bright green color with a white or pinkish base and have 1–6 prominent, parallel veins running the length of the leaf.

FLOWERS: Flowers are tiny and densely arranged on a spadix that emerges approximately at the midpoint of a sheath that closely resembles the leaves. The spadix is up to 9 cm long and 1 cm wide. Individual flowers are about 3 mm across and have white- or tan-colored tepals, yellow anthers, and a green ovary.

FRUITS: The fruit is a tiny, 3-celled, pyramidal-shaped, gelatinous berry containing 5–7 ovoid seeds around 3 mm long.

ROOTS: The root system is shallow and branching. Rhizomes are brown with a white interior and are somewhat zig-zagged in shape.

DISTRIBUTION AND HABITAT

While there is some taxonomic confusion regarding how many species of *Acorus* are in North America, it is generally accepted that there are two very similar species, *A. americanus* and *A. calamus*. The primary differences between the two are that *A. calamus* is sterile, doesn't produce fruits, is slightly larger on average, and is considered non-native. The species are distributed primarily in North America's northern and eastern parts. *Acorus americanus* is found mainly in the northern half of the U.S. up to Alaska and the Northwest Territories of Canada. *Acorus calamus* is more widely distributed, primarily east of the Rocky Mountains, from Texas to Quebec. Both species grow along the edges of ponds and lakes, and in marshes, in water up to 0.5 m deep.

FORAGING

The young flower stalk and underground rhizome of Sweet Flag can be peeled and eaten raw. A sweet, dried preserve can be made from rhizomes by cutting them into small, uniform pieces and boiling them (changing out the water several times) for at least 20 minutes. The boiling process helps to remove bitterness and improve the flavor. The boiled roots should be simmered in sugar syrup for 20 minutes. After drying, these can be stored in a cool, dry place for up to six months.

Sweet Flag is mostly known for its wide array of medicinal properties across many herbal traditions. A common theme is the use of Sweet Flag as a treatment for digestive ailments and to stimulate the appetite, similar to ginger. It is also used to treat memory disorders and as a nerve tonic. Additionally, it can support smoking cessation, as chewing the roots (dried or fresh) makes smoking unpalatable.

Sweet Flag has a refreshing, lemony-sweet smell when you crush the leaves, which can help you distinguish it from plants with similar leaves.

QUICK REFERENCE:

USES: edible, medicinal

FORAGE SEASON(S): spring

FORAGE PART(S): young flower stalk, rhizomes

SPECIAL CONCERNS: *Iris* is a poisonous look-alike. Sweet Flag varieties from Europe, Russia, Japan, and India may contain carcinogenic alkylbenzenes.

AGRIMONY
STICKLEWORT
CHURCH STEEPLES
FAIRY'S WAND

Agrimonia spp.

PLANT: Herbaceous, upright perennials with stout, hairy stems. Plants may reach 150 cm in height.

LEAVES: Alternate, pinnately divided leaves. Leaflets are lanceolate with serrated edges.

FLOWERS: In terminal and axillary racemes of 9–120 flowers. Individual flowers have five ovular, yellow petals. The base of each flower is surrounded by a cup-shaped tube called a hypanthium, with 2–5 rows of bristles on its outer surface.

FRUITS: At maturity, the hypanthium enlarges, becomes bell- or top-shaped, and is typically grooved. Within each hypanthium is one achene.

ROOTS: Roots are either fibrous or thickened and tuberous.

DISTRIBUTION AND HABITAT

The genus *Agrimonia* includes over 20 species, with seven species distributed through-out North America, though notably more prevalent in the eastern half. It grows in forest margins and roadside ditches.

FORAGING

Agrimony is a medicinal herb, tea, dye, and "famine food." There is a fascinating and varied historical record of Agrimony being used to treat everything from gout to snake bites. According to multiple secondary records citing 18th century Scottish Witch Trials, Agrimony was a magical remedy for "elf-shot," an unexplained and sudden illness or pain believed to be caused by invisible elves with invisible arrows. The common name, "Fairy's Wands," is likely due to the numerous references to the magical properties of Agrimony found in historical texts. In more modern medicinal applications, Agrimony leaves are dried and prepared as a tea that is applied topically to treat minor skin irritations and internally to treat minor ailments such as sore throats.

Fresh leaves and stems are harvested, finely chopped, and steeped in a water bath to create a yellow-green dye. Outcomes vary based on the mordant (color fixative) used and the time of year plant material is harvested.

A frequently cited translation of an ancient Chinese text on edible plants refers to Agrimony as a "famine food when all else fails." It describes the process of preparing flour from dried and ground seeds.

QUICK REFERENCE

USES: edible, dye, medicinal
FORAGE SEASON(S): spring, summer, fall
FORAGE PART(S): leaves, seeds
SPECIAL CONCERNS: none

GARLIC MUSTARD
POOR MAN'S MUSTARD
HEDGE MUSTARD

Alliaria petiolata

PLANT: Herbaceous biennial, producing only basal leaves in its first year, reaching up to 1.2 m in height in its second year. All parts of the plant emit a garlic-like odor, especially noticeable when crushed.

LEAVES: First-year leaves are kidney- or heart-shaped, up to 6 cm long and wide, with scalloped edges and a somewhat wrinkly-appearing surface. Second-year leaves are similarly shaped but larger (up to 9 cm), with the margins bearing larger, rounded teeth. Leaves decrease in size as you go up the stem and tend to become more triangular.

FLOWERS: Flowers are borne in many-flowered racemes at the stem tips. Individual flowers are up to 1 cm across and have four white, ovoid petals surrounding short, greenish stamens.

FRUITS: A thin, cylindrical pod (silique) up to 5 cm long. The pods usually curve upwards. The seeds are dark brown or black, oblong in shape, and 2–5 mm long.

ROOTS: A taproot with a distinctive L- or S-shaped curve near the soil surface.

DISTRIBUTION AND HABITAT

Garlic Mustard is a widespread and harmful invasive species that can poison plants in its vicinity, resulting in it being the only species present (monoculture). It is currently found primarily in the eastern half of North America, about as far south as central Alabama. It is widely scattered in the western half of North America, from Edmonton, Alberta, to Los Angeles, California. It tends to be found in wooded or partially wooded areas and is especially common along trails.

FORAGING

Garlic Mustard was likely brought to North America by European settlers who used it for food and medicine. It is an excellent forage plant because it is an invasive species. Any removal or reduction of the population is beneficial because it is widespread. It is also easy to identify based on appearance and odor, and has edible parts in multiple seasons. In early spring, the young leaves and shoots can be used directly in salads. Slightly older leaves are often chopped and treated like a pesto sauce for noodles. Seeds can be added to loaves of bread and savory baked goods or soaked in vinegar and used to make mustard. Taproots can be harvested and used like horseradish roots. Garlic Mustard is no

longer commonly used by most foragers for medicinal purposes. Still, European settlers reportedly used it for various ailments, including treating intestinal parasites and cleansing wounds.

QUICK REFERENCE:

USES: edible, medicinal
FORAGE SEASON(S): spring, summer, fall
FORAGE PART(S): roots, stems, leaves, flowers, seeds
SPECIAL CONCERNS: none

AMARANTH

Amaranthus spp.

PLANT: A diverse group of mostly annual herbaceous plants or shrubs. They may be erect, decumbent (sprawling on the ground, with the stem tips erect), or prostrate (lying completely flat on the ground), and are typically well-branched.

LEAVES: Alternate in arrangement, a variety of leaf shapes can be found within *Amaranthus*, ranging from linear to lanceolate, spatulate (spoon-shaped), ovulate, or rhombic (diamond-shaped). In most species, the leaf margin is entire, with some species having wavy or undulate margins.

FLOWERS: Flowers are in terminal or axillary spikes, panicles, or glomerules (ball-shaped clusters of flowers). They are unisexual, with individual species being either monoecious or dioecious. Individual flowers usually have 3–5 translucent to greenish tepals up to 4 mm long. Flowering components are often subtended (beneath the flower) by reduced leaves or bracts.

FRUITS: Fruits are utricles (dry, one-seeded fruits surrounded by a thin, membranous covering) loosely contained within the inner tepals. Each utricle contains one seed that is globular to lenticular in shape and usually smooth and shiny. The seed is enclosed in the pericarp (fruit covering originating from the ovary wall), which generally has a seam around the middle, which leads to the top half falling off, exposing the seed within.

ROOTS: Most species have a taproot (often deep), from which a secondary, fibrous root system spreads.

DISTRIBUTION AND HABITAT

Over 75 *Amaranthus* species are distributed across all continents except Antarctica; 38 can be found in North America, with many of these being non-native. Amaranth can be found in many habitats but is most common in areas with disturbance, such as yards, roadsides, riverbanks, lakeshores, and railroad tracks. Like *Chenopodium*, some species can be found throughout most of North America, while others have a more limited range.

FORAGING

All parts of all *Amaranthus* species are edible. Anthropological and archaeological records suggest that it has been an important cultivated crop across the globe for more than 10,000 years. It is most often cultivated or foraged for its high-protein, nutrient-dense seeds. Harvest seeds when plants naturally begin to senesce (wither away and die) at the end of the growing season. Seed heads can be clipped off and stored in paper bags for drying. After several weeks, seeds will drop off the heads and can be separated from the remaining plant material. After drying, seeds can be stored for up to six months, ground for flour, or cooked like a cereal grain, such as oatmeal. Some foragers prepare the Amaranth seeds like popcorn and eat them as snack food. *Amaranthus* plants can provide nutritious food throughout the growing season; young leaves and stems can be eaten raw or cooked. Older leaves and stems can also be consumed but will not be tender and may have a bitter taste.

Some *Amaranthus* species provide valuable dyes. The flowers and bracts of *A. cruentus*, commonly known as Hopi Red Dye Amaranth or Komo, are steeped in water overnight to extract soluble dyes that are added to traditional Hopi foods and used to dye fabric. Dye created from Amaranth is considered safe for consumption, but artificially prepared red dye, known as Red No. 2 or Amaranth (referencing the color but made from petroleum byproducts), is banned by the FDA in the United States as a carcinogen. The Red Dye No. 2 scare caused the Mars candy factory to remove red M&Ms from the mix for most of the 1980s—despite the fact that they never contained Red Dye No. 2.

QUICK REFERENCE

USES: edible, dye
FORAGE SEASON(S): spring, summer (leaves), fall (seeds)
FORAGE PART(S): leaves, seeds
SPECIAL CONCERNS: none

JUNEBERRY
SERVICEBERRY
SHADBLOW
SHADBUSH
SASKATOON

Amelanchier spp.

PLANT: Deciduous shrubs and small trees in the Rose family, ranging in height from 0.2 m to 25 m. Individual plants can have 1–150 erect stems depending on the species. The bark is typically gray or brown and smooth or fissured. Many species often form colonies through suckering or rhizomatous growth.

LEAVES: Leaves are alternate in arrangement and simple, usually with an elliptical or ovate shape, up to 10 cm long and 5 cm wide, with either entire, serrate, or dentate margins. The upper and lower leaf surfaces may be hairy.

FLOWERS: Flowers are terminal and arranged either in clusters of up to four flowers or racemes bearing up to 20 flowers. Individual flowers are up to 55 mm wide, with five petals that are usually white, rarely pinkish. There are 7–28 stamens shorter than or equal to the petals in length and 2–6 styles.

FRUITS: Fruit is a globose pome (pear-shaped in one species), up to 15 mm in diameter, often with the sepals persisting on the outer surface, and containing no more than a few seeds (sometimes no seeds are present). Ripe fruit color ranges from pink to blue to purple to black, depending on the species. Some species have sweet fruit, while some have less flavorful fruit.

ROOTS: Large root systems are formed, usually as wide as the tree's canopy. The trees produce a thick, dense mat of thick roots just below the soil surface.

DISTRIBUTION AND HABITAT

In North America, *Amelanchier* species can be found in every state (except Hawaii) and every Canadian province, though they are the least abundant in the Midwest. There are approximately 20 species, but species identification can be problematic because there is variability within species, and the species are known to hybridize with each other readily. Typical habitats are quite variable amongst the species, with at least one species seemingly adapted to most habitat types found across the U.S. and Canada.

FORAGING

Despite its name, the fruits of the Juneberry are not true berries but pomes, like apples.

Juneberries ripen in June to early July and are easy to identify and pick. They can be consumed raw or processed in a variety of ways. The pomes naturally contain pectin and make a good preserve. Juneberry fruits were commonly used in pemmican, small cakes of lean meat, berries, and lard, first developed and used by Indigenous people of the Northern Woodlands and Plains as a high-calorie food for long-distance travel and survival. European colonizers and even arctic explorers later co-opted pemmican for their adventures.

QUICK REFERENCE:

USES: edible
FORAGE SEASON(S): summer
FORAGE PART(S): fruit
SPECIAL CONCERNS: none

SASKATOON SERVICEBERRY
JUNEBERRY
WESTERN SERVICEBERRY

Amelanchier
species of
interest

Amelanchier alnifolia

KEY FEATURES

The Saskatoon Serviceberry is a shrub with showy white flowers in the spring. It produces berries that are dark purple when ripe. The bark is brown with reddish-brown stems. It is smaller than most other serviceberries (the fruit of trees and shrubs in the Rose family) reaching up to 5 m tall.

DOWNY SERVICEBERRY
SHADBUSH
COMMON SERVICEBERRY

Amelanchier
species of
interest

Amelanchier arborea

KEY FEATURES

The Downy Serviceberry is a shrub or tree with showy white flowers. It is considered to be the best-tasting of the *Amelanchier* species. When ripe, berries are bright red to dark purple. Bark is gray with lighter vertical stripes. It can reach up to 10 m tall.

CANADIAN SERVICEBERRY
SHADBLOW SERVICEBERRY

Amelanchier canadensis

KEY FEATURES

The Canadian Serviceberry is a shrub or small tree with showy white flowers. Its graceful and delicate dome form distinguishes it from other *Amelanchier* species. Berries are purple to black when ripe. Bark is gray with darker vertical stripes. It can reach up to 8 m tall.

HOG PEANUT
WILD PEANUT
GROUND BEAN

Amphicarpaea bracteata

PLANT: An herbaceous, branching, annual, or short-lived perennial vine in the Pea family, reaching lengths of up to 1.5 m. The plant lacks tendrils and climbs by coiling around neighboring vegetation.

LEAVES: The alternate leaves are compound and comprised of three broad, oval-shaped leaflets. The middle leaflet is held on a much longer stalk than the other two leaflets. Individual leaflets can grow up to 7 cm long and 6 cm wide and typically turn gold or yellow in the fall.

FLOWERS: Hog Peanut is noteworthy for having two different kinds of flowers (and fruits). On the upper parts of the stems, it bears typical pea-like flowers that hang in loose racemes. Each flower is approximately 1.5 cm in length and is colored from white to pink to pale purple. The other type of flower is produced on the lower parts of the stems and lateral branches. These flowers lack petals and never open and self-pollinate, a cleistogamous flower. They are typically found on or just beneath the soil surface.

FRUITS: The pea-like flowers produce flat, oblong pods, like a pea pod. Pods typically contain 3–4 ballistically dispersed seeds when the pod splits open. The cleistogamous flowers make a fleshy one-seeded pod that buries itself like a peanut.

ROOTS: Hog Peanut shoots grow from a shallow taproot. Bacteria form nodules on the roots, fixing atmospheric nitrogen to a form the plant can readily uptake.

DISTRIBUTION AND HABITAT

Hog Peanut is found almost entirely in the eastern half of the United States and adjacent portions of Canada. It is usually found in at least partially shady areas with moist soil, such as woodland edges, along trails, and wet meadows and prairies.

FORAGING

Hog Peanut is so named because wild pigs dig up and consume the pods that form from the subterranean, cleistogamous flower. Hog Peanut is unique because it produces two types of fruit: the larger, single-seeded pod found underground and a typical above-ground bean pod. This plant is very common and an aggressive spreader. Hog Peanut is a nitrogen-fixing plant and contributes to the health of the soil and the surrounding plants. Bean pods and underground pods can be harvested from late summer to fall. The beans can be eaten raw or prepared like other lentils.

QUICK REFERENCE:

USES: edible, nitrogen-fixing
FORAGE SEASON(S): late summer, fall
FORAGE PART(S): fruit
SPECIAL CONCERNS: none

HOPNISS
AMERICAN GROUNDNUT
AMERICAN HODOIMO
CINNAMON VINE
POTATO BEAN

Apios americana

PLANT: An herbaceous perennial vine that can grow up to 6 m in length, usually seen climbing up trees or over shrubs and herbaceous vegetation.

LEAVES: Leaves are alternate and pinnately compound, with 5–7 leaflets. Leaflets may be glabrous (without hairs) or pubescent (covered with short, soft hairs) and ovate to lanceolate, with a rounded base, a pointed tip, and an entire margin. They range in size from 2–10 cm in length and 1.5–4 cm in width.

FLOWERS: Flowers are borne in axillary racemes, usually dense clusters of 5–10 flowers. They tend to be less dense in the Southern parts of their range. Flowers are irregular in shape, somewhat reminiscent of a typical pea flower. While they have five petals, they are specialized in their structure and not easily discernible. The single upper petal (the banner) is large and appears divided into two "wings." The banner is pale on the outside and reddish-brown inside. Two adjacent petals (the wings) are purplish-brown and surround the two bottom petals (the keel), which are partially fused and form a curved or coiled boat-shaped structure, pinkish-white in color.

FRUITS: The fruit is a legume, a bean-like pod that splits open along a seam on two sides. They are up to 12 cm long and 6 mm wide and hold up to 12 seeds per pod. Seeds are irregularly shaped with a wrinkled surface, up to 5 mm long. They are colored green initially, turning dark brown when mature.

ROOTS: Roots are thin and rhizomatous, bearing two or more tubers in a series, like beads on a string. The tubers are up to 6 cm in diameter.

DISTRIBUTION AND HABITAT

This species is found throughout the eastern half of North America, from southern Canada to southern Florida. It is usually found in damp thickets or woods, often near the shores of open bodies of water.

FORAGING

The seeds and tubers of Hopniss are edible and nutritious. However, there are some reports of indigestion and stomach discomfort following consumption in some individu-

als. The tubers are particularly important, containing more than twice the protein of cultivated potato (*Solanum tuberosum*) and higher calcium levels, niacin, and other vitamins and minerals. Hopniss was an important food source for Indigenous people throughout North America, and some intentional cultivation was practiced across North America as early as 8000 BCE. The extent and duration of this practice are highly debated. Early European colonizers of North America learned to use Hopniss from observing Indigenous people. The Pilgrims almost certainly survived their first several winters, largely thanks to the Wampanoag People sharing their knowledge and cultural practice of preserving and eating Hopniss.

Tubers can be harvested at any time of the year, but the largest tubers will be found in the fall, and harvest is easiest after the first frost has killed back the large vines. The underground tubers are typically located within a 0.5 m radius of where the main stem meets the soil and are usually no deeper than 15 cm. Tubers form in a chain. They may range in size from a raisin to a baseball—reports of much larger and more abundant tubers are made but not verified. Upon harvest, tubers can be dried and ground as flour, roasted, boiled, or fried. Eating raw tubers is not advisable.

QUICK REFERENCE

USES: edible

FORAGE SEASON(S): summer, fall

FORAGE PART(S): seeds, tubers

SPECIAL CONCERNS: Do not consume raw seeds or tubers.

QUICK REFERENCE:

USES: edible
FORAGE SEASON(S): spring, summer, fall
FORAGE PART(S): roots, sometimes young leaves
SPECIAL CONCERNS: none

BURDOCK ROOT

Arctium spp.

PLANT: Herbaceous biennials or monocarpic perennials (die after flowering) with erect, ascending, branching stems that can reach up to 2 m in height.

LEAVES: Leaves are alternately arranged on long, usually hollow petioles. The leaves are large, coarse, and heart-shaped, up to 70 cm long, resembling rhubarb leaves. Basal leaves are the largest, with the stem leaves gradually becoming smaller as you move up the stem. Upper leaf surfaces are usually dotted with glands, while the lower leaf surface is generally tomentose (densely covered with matted hairs).

FLOWERS: Borne in leafy panicles, racemes, or corymbs. They are of the composite type and globular in overall shape. Each composite head is comprised of 5–40+ pink-purple florets. Surrounding the base of the flower are numerous, dense, spiny bracts, each with a hooked tip.

FRUITS: Fruits are cypselae, a dry, single-seeded fruit. The bracts dry to brown and readily fall off, with the hooked tip readily attaching to fur and clothing, like Velcro.

ROOTS: Typically, a massive taproot is up to 120 cm long.

DISTRIBUTION AND HABITAT

Ten species native to Eurasia and Africa have been introduced worldwide. In North America, three species are present and can be found in various habitats, from sunny fields to ditches to woodlands, often in disturbed or neglected areas.

FORAGING

Most people in North America only see Burdock as an annoying, burr-producing weed, commonly observed along walking trails and other disturbed areas. However, the roots and young leaves of the first-year Burdock plant are edible, and in some parts of the world, Burdock is cultivated as a commonly used root crop. Burdock is a biennial that completes its life cycle over two growing seasons. In the first year, it stores energy in the form of carbohydrates in its roots in preparation for year two, when it will form a flower stalk and eventually produce the annoying burrs we try to avoid! While not poisonous, second-year roots and leaves are bitter and fibrous and should not be harvested. Roots from first-year plants can be collected as early in the season as desired until late fall. Harvested roots should be thoroughly cleaned and can be eaten raw or prepared in any fashion. Roots are often included in stir fry and soups or are roasted. North American Burdock has a more bitter, earthy taste than cultivated Burdock and is tastier when cooked as opposed to eaten raw.

GREATER BURDOCK
BEGGAR'S BUTTONS

Arctium
species of
interest

Arctium lappa

KEY FEATURES

Greater Burdock is a large, herbaceous biennial with burs. It is distinguished from
A. minus by being generally larger overall, including larger flowers on longer, more
branched stems. Greater Burdock reaches a maximum height of about 3 m.

LESSER BURDOCK
LITTLE BURDOCK
CUCKOO-BUTTON

Arctium
species of
interest

Arctium minus

KEY FEATURES

Lesser Burdock is an herbaceous biennial with burs. It can be distinguished from *A. lappa* by the presence of hollow stems in the lower leaves and sessile or short-stalked flowers. Lesser Burdock reaches a maximum height of about 2 m.

MUGWORT
WORMWOOD
SAGEBRUSH

Artemisia spp.

PLANT: A large, diverse group of biennials, perennials, subshrubs, and shrubs, up to 3.5 m in height, in the Aster family. Most species are aromatic to some degree and are used as flavorings in various foods and drinks, as well as in products such as candles and incense.

LEAVES: Leaves are alternate in arrangement and may be grass-like, lanceolate, elliptical, ovate, or spatulate (spoon-shaped) in shape. Many species have lobed leaves, sometimes very prominently, resulting in a fern or feather-like appearance. All species produce basal leaves, and some have stem leaves.

FLOWERS: Flowers are typically tiny, inconspicuous, and button-shaped, and lack petals or ray flowers, consisting entirely of disc flowers. They are borne in broad panicles or in narrow racemes or spikes. Flower color is generally whitish to yellowish to greenish, with a few red-flowered species.

FRUITS: Brown, spindle-shaped cypselae (single-seeded fruits) that are often gland-dotted. In most species, they do not have any hairs to aid in wind dispersal.

ROOTS: They often have extensive root systems that facilitate vegetative reproduction and spread.

DISTRIBUTION AND HABITAT

There are around 500 species of *Artemisia* worldwide, approximately 60 of which may be found in North America. As a whole, they can be found nearly throughout North America. A large number of species are adapted to dry or harsh environments, such as salt flats, steppe, tundra, and desert. There are exceptions, however, with some species adapted to more mesic or wet environments.

FORAGING

Although *Artemisia* was more recently discovered by modern science as a literal and figurative medical goldmine, it has been used in traditional and folk medicine for millennia to treat worms and other parasites. *Artemisia* species have known anthelmintic properties and most folk remedies involve drinking tea prepared from dried leaves. The compound Artemisinin found in some *Artemisia* species is effective against both parasitic worms and the protozoan that causes malaria. In 2015, Dr. Tu Youyou, a pharmaceutical chemist and protozoan expert, was awarded the Nobel Prize in medicine for her profoundly important work in discovering this compound and developing treatments for malaria that have saved millions of lives. This is not a forage plant recommended for use by novices but under the guidance of an expert herbalist or traditional healer.

QUICK REFERENCE:

USES: medicinal, recreational

FORAGE SEASON(S): spring, summer, fall

FORAGE PART(S): leaves

SPECIAL CONCERNS: It contains the neurotoxin thujone.

ABSINTHE WORMWOOD

Artemisia absinthium

KEY FEATURES

Absinthe Wormwood is a non-native herbaceous perennial weed with fern-like leaves. It is highly aromatic and, more specifically, known for its use in several different alcoholic beverages, most famously absinthe, a very popular drink of the early 20th-century counter-culture. Absinthe was ultimately banned due to prohibitionist rhetoric and dubious science—but made a resurgence in the late 20th century when it was legalized.

MUGWORT

Artemisia vulgaris

KEY FEATURES

Mugwort is a non-native herbaceous to somewhat woody perennial weed with silvery, finely cut leaves. *Artemisia vulgaris*, sometimes referred to as the "mother of herbs," is a rich source of bioactive compounds used in numerous traditional medicines and was recently used in several patented pharmaceuticals.

WINTERCRESS
YELLOW ROCKET
BITTERCRESS

Barbarea vulgaris

PLANT: Herbaceous biennial (rarely perennial) up to 1 m tall. The stems are noticeably ribbed, and the entire plant lacks hairs.

LEAVES: It has a basal rosette of pinnately compound, lyre-shaped leaves up to 10 cm long, with the terminal lobe being the largest, and 1–4 pairs of smaller lobes on each side of the stalk. Stem leaves are alternate and become smaller up the stem, with the lowest leaves resembling the basal leaves. Upper stem leaves are usually stalkless and wedge-shaped with or without shallow lobes. Stem leaves typically have a pair of lobes at the base that clasps the stem. All leaves have a dark green, glossy appearance.

FLOWERS: Flowers are borne in roundish clusters, about 4 cm across, at the top of the stem. Individual flowers are approximately 0.75 cm wide and consist of four yellow, strap-shaped petals, six anthers, and a slender style. The flower clusters elongate during the blooming period, with flowers gradually opening at the tip as the cluster expands, seed pods gradually forming beneath them.

FRUITS: The fruits are slender, cylindrical pods, 1–3 cm long. They tend to angle or curve upwards. Within each pod are numerous oblong, dark brown seeds, about 1.5 mm long.

ROOTS: A stout taproot with fibrous secondary roots.

DISTRIBUTION AND HABITAT

Wintercress is a native of Eurasia and North Africa. It has naturalized across much of the United States and Southern Canada, especially in the Midwest and eastward. A nearly identical native species, *B. orthoceras*, has a more northern and western distribution. *B. vulgaris* is primarily found in disturbed habitats with moist soil, such as ditches, along the edges of waterbodies, wet meadows, and waste places.

FORAGING

Wintercress is a great forage plant to get to know because it is an introduced species and an invasive weed in some parts of North America. It is also one of the earliest greens available in the north. All that aside, Wintercress has a strong, bitter flavor, and some consider it nearly unpalatable. Very young leaves and unopened flower buds can be eaten raw, but older leaves should be boiled with several water changes to reduce bitter flavors. An abundance of this forage plant is available, and it is an exotic species, so you

can experiment with preparation strategies and not be overly concerned about waste. Despite its strong taste, it is a healthy green, available when other forage options might be limited.

QUICK REFERENCE:

USES: edible

FORAGE SEASON(S): spring, summer, late winter

FORAGE PART(S): leaves

SPECIAL CONCERNS: none

BARBERRY

Berberis spp.

PLANT: A large genus of shrubs, ranging from 1–8 m. Shoots are considered dimorphic, having both long shoots and short shoots. The long shoots, which are the main shoots/stems of the shrub, have leaves modified into spines. A short shoot develops from the axil of each spine, which contains the typical leaves. Some horticulturists separate some species of *Berberis* into the genus *Mahonia* (Oregon Grape). *Mahonia* differs by lacking spines and having compound leaves. Most botanists, however, do not recognize *Mahonia* as a valid genus.

LEAVES: Leaves are simple and alternate in arrangement, although they often appear whorled. The leaf shape is ovate to spatulate (spoon-shaped) to lanceolate, up to 5 cm long and 1.5 cm wide. Depending on the species, leaf margins may be lobed or toothed, with bristles or short spines at the tips.

FLOWERS: Flowers are found on short shoots, either solitary or formed in racemes or loose clusters. The coloration typically is some shade of yellow or orange. Individual flowers are small (<8 mm), with most species having six petals and the others having three or nine.

FRUITS: Fruit is a round or oval-shaped berry, usually around 1 cm long. Depending on the species, the ripe berries are either red or blue, often covered with a waxy bloom, and may be dry or juicy. Within each fruit are 1–10 brownish to blackish seeds.

ROOTS: A thick mass of fibrous roots initially develops, followed by the growth of rhizomes, which eventually create new shoots.

DISTRIBUTION AND HABITAT

There are about 500 *Berberis* species native to many parts of the world, with several species introduced outside their native ranges, often becoming invasive. In North America, 22 species are present. Preferred habitats are variable, depending on the species. They are distributed throughout North America, often in open woodland or grassland areas.

FORAGING

Barberry is not a widely foraged food crop in North America, but it is used in some Persian and Indian dishes, primarily as dried fruit. Barberry fruit can be harvested in fall or winter, as ripe fruit stays on the plant. The fruit naturally contains pectin and can be used to make jams and jellies or dried. All *Berberis* species are edible, but different species have different flavor profiles, ranging from cranberry-like to slightly sweeter.

The berries also contain the alkaloid berberine, which is used to treat certain cardiovascular and metabolic disorders. Roots can be used to produce a vivid chartreuse dye.

QUICK REFERENCE:

USES: edible, dye, medicinal

FORAGE SEASON(S): fall, winter

FORAGE PART(S): fruit, root

SPECIAL CONCERNS: Barberry is easy to identify and distinguish from other red berry-producing shrubs, but it is always a good idea to review plants that produce poisonous red fruit in the fall to confirm identification further. The fruit contains the alkaloid berberine and should be consumed in moderation.

OREGON GRAPE
MAHONIA

Berberis aquifolium (Synonym: *Mahonia aquifolium*)

KEY FEATURES

Oregon Grape is an evergreen shrub with leaves that look similar to Holly (*Ilex*). Like all members of the *Berberis* genus, the fruits contain the alkaloid berberine. It is harvested and used like grapes (*Vitis*).

BIRCH

Betula spp.

PLANT: Multi-trunked shrubs and trees. They are mostly known for their bark, which can be reddish brown, yellowish, or white. It displays prominent horizontal lenticels, and usually exfoliates into papery strips on older specimens. They are known to hybridize, making species identification difficult in areas with more than one species.

LEAVES: Leaves are typically two-ranked and grow from spur-like branchlets on the twigs. Leaf shape, depending on the species, is ovate or deltate. Most species have prominently serrated leaf margins, with a few having crenate or lobed margins. Upper and lower surfaces range from hairless to tomentose (densely covered by wooly, matted hairs), with some species having glandular hairs on the lower surface.

FLOWERS: *Betula* are monoecious, having separate male and female flowers on the same plant. Male and female flowers are both in the form of catkins, a dense, cylindrical cluster of inconspicuous flowers, often hanging or drooping from the twig. Male catkins appear on the tips of branches and are formed in the fall, persisting as a rigid catkin during the winter, opening with the leaves next spring. Female catkins are erect and solitary, growing from the branchlets on each twig.

FRUITS: *Betula* produce samaras, an achene with a papery wing of tissue that forms from the ovary wall. The wings allow the seeds to travel further in the wind.

ROOTS: Large root systems are formed, usually as wide as the tree's canopy. The trees produce a thick, dense mat of thick roots just below the soil surface.

DISTRIBUTION AND HABITAT

Betula includes a group of 35 species (18 in North America). Birches are primarily found in the northern temperate and boreal regions of the Northern Hemisphere. Most species tend to be found in cool and moist habitats or microclimates, such as bogs, river/lake shorelines, cool and damp woodlands, and on north-facing slopes in the warmer parts of its range.

FORAGING

The sap of Birch trees can be collected using the same techniques employed to gather Maple sap. Birch sap is the sweetest in the month before leaf emergence. Birch sap can be consumed as is or processed into Birch syrup, Birch beer, or similar products. Birch syrup and Maple syrup are prepared using the same process but are distinct products with different flavor profiles. It requires twice the sap to produce Birch syrup. Birch beer can be made from sap or syrup in either an alcoholic or non-alcoholic version, depending on the method employed.

HICKORY
PECAN

Carya spp.

PLANT: A group of trees and a few shrubs in the Walnut family (Juglandaceae). The tallest species can attain heights of 50 m. Individual trees in a given area can be highly variable in outward appearance, suggesting hybridization commonly occurs between species.

LEAVES: Pinnately compound, with 3–21 leaflets, depending on the species. The outer leaflets are usually the largest and can be up to 26 cm long and 14 cm wide. Leaflet shapes range from elliptical to obovate. The lower leaf surface in all species has both hairs and scales. Upper leaf surfaces in all species are similarly covered in hairs and scales but often fall off during the growing season, appearing glabrous by autumn.

FLOWERS: *Carya* are monoecious. Male flowers are sessile or hanging catkins on 1- to 2-year-old stems. Female flowers are borne on the tips of current-year branches in spikes of 2–4. Both male and female flowers are typically colored yellowish to greenish.

FRUITS: Fruits are brownish to tannish-colored nuts. They are enclosed in a husk that either partially or completely splits open at maturity.

ROOTS: Large root systems are formed, usually as wide as the tree's canopy. The trees produce a thick, dense mat of thick roots just below the soil surface.

DISTRIBUTION AND HABITAT

Carya species range from southern Canada to Central America. They are most abundant in the eastern hardwood forests of the U.S. They tend to be found in hardwood forests with either dry or mesic soil moisture conditions.

FORAGING

The common name "Hickory" is believed to be derived from the Virginia Algonquian word "pawcohiccora," a nut butter prepared by pounding nuts with water. English colonizers later associated the term describing the food with the tree from which the nuts originated. There are several species of Hickory. All are easy to identify and edible, although the Pignut Hickory, *Carya glabra*, is quite bitter and said to be fit only for animals. However, it is safe to consume, and the bitterness will leech out if harvested later in the season. The Pignut Hickory is so named because the nut, when halved, resembles a pig snout. Despite a few species with a bitter flavor profile, most Hickory nuts are delicious and worth the effort to harvest. Nuts fall to the ground around the time leaves change color and fall

from the tree. The tedious part of Hickory harvest is extracting nutmeat from the shell. The most direct method is to open nuts and pick out the nutmeat with a nutpick. Several additional processing strategies can be employed.

QUICK REFERENCE:

USES: edible

FORAGE SEASON(S): late summer to fall

FORAGE PART(S): fruit

SPECIAL CONCERNS: none

PECAN

Carya illinoinensis

KEY FEATURES

Pecan is a large deciduous tree with pinnately compound leaves bearing 11–17 leaflets. It is the largest of the Hickory trees, with a broad crown up to 50 m tall. Fruits are desired forage foods because they have a thin shell with easy-to-access, oily nutmeat. Pecans are primarily found in the lower Mississippi river valley.

SHELLBARK HICKORY

Carya laciniosa

KEY FEATURES

Shellbark Hickory is a large, deciduous tree with pinnately compound leaves bearing 5–9 leaflets. The bark is shaggy and gray, like *C. ovata*. Edible nuts have the thickest shells compared to *C. illinoinensis* and *C. ovata*. Nutmeat is sweet and oily. Shellbark Hickory is broadly distributed across the Northeast and much of the Midwest.

SHAGBARK HICKORY

Carya ovata

KEY FEATURES

Shagbark Hickory is a deciduous tree with pinnately compound leaves bearing 3–5 leaflets. It can be distinguished from *C. laciniosa* by having fewer leaflets per leaf and smaller leaflets. It also produces a smaller nut with a thinner shell. Shagbark Hickory is distributed throughout the eastern United States and southeastern Canada.

NEW JERSEY TEA
REDROOT
SOAP BUSH
CALIFORNIA LILAC

Ceanothus americanus

PLANT: A genus of mostly shrubs and small, multi-trunked trees. Shrubby species rarely exceed 3 m in height, while the few treelike species can get up to 7 m. The inner root bark of most species is red.

LEAVES: Most species are evergreen, with the deciduous species found in the colder parts of its range. Leaves are typically small and simple with toothed margins. Both alternate- and opposite-leaved species occur.

FLOWERS: Tiny, fragrant flowers are borne in terminal or axillary dense, cyme-like clusters. Flowers are perfect (bisexu-al), with five (occasionally six) petals, 6–8 stamens, and 3–4 styles. Petal color ranges from white to blue to pink to purple, depending on the species.

FRUITS: Fruits are hard, three-sectioned, nut-like capsules, usually triangular. Each section contains one seed.

ROOTS: Most, if not all, species develop a deep taproot with widely spreading lateral roots.

DISTRIBUTION AND HABITAT

There are 50–60 species of *Ceanothus* that can be found in North America, from Central America to Southern Canada, and from the West Coast to the East Coast. Most species are found in the western part of the U.S., especially California, with only three species found east of the Rocky Mountains. Species identification can be problematic in the western parts of its range due to local and geographic variability and widespread hybridization. Most species prefer dry and at least somewhat open habitats, such as chaparral (evergreen shrub plant community), rocky slopes, pine-oak woodlands, sandhills, and dry prairies.

FORAGING

English colonizers of North America adopted several *Ceanothus* spp. as suitable substitutes for English tea that was made unavailable during the American Revolutionary War. Later, during the American Civil War, Chinese tea access was exorbitantly expensive, and New Jersey Tea regained popularity as a substitute. Colonizers most likely adopted the

use from local Indigenous people who may have used the roots prepared as a tea for a broad range of medicinal applications, including staunching blood loss following childbirth and other uses.

Tea made from dried or fresh leaves has a pleasant and slightly minty flavor, with some claiming it has mild sedative properties.

QUICK REFERENCE:

USES: edible, medicinal

FORAGE SEASON(S): spring, summer, fall

FORAGE PART(S): leaves, bark

SPECIAL CONCERNS: Some *Ceanothus* spp. are toxic.

HACKBERRY
SUGARBERRY

Celtis spp.

PLANT: A genus of mostly trees, with a few shrub species, in the Ulmaceae family. They are generally mid-sized trees (<30 m in height), with either smooth or noticeably warty bark.

LEAVES: Leaves are alternate in arrangement and simple in overall form. Leaf shape tends to be deltate to ovate, often with a pointed tip and serrated leaf margins.

FLOWERS: This is a monoecious group, with separate male and female flowers on the same plant. Occasionally, bisexual flowers can be found. Individual flowers are small (<1 cm wide) with 4–6 greenish to yellowish sepals and no petals. Male flowers are borne in cymes or fascicles near the base of first-year branches and have 4–6 stamens. Female flowers are usually solitary or in few-flowered clusters, growing from the leaf axils near the tips of first-year branches. They have 4–5 rudimentary, non-functional stamens and one two-parted style.

FRUITS: A round to oval-shaped fleshy drupe containing one seed. They ripen in autumn and often persist well after leaf fall.

ROOTS: Roots are woody, deep, and extend past the tree dripline (crown circumference).

DISTRIBUTION AND HABITAT

Celtis spp. are distributed throughout most North America, from southern Canada to the Caribbean Islands and Panama. They are a common component of many types of forested habitats throughout their range.

FORAGING

Hackberry produces one of the more nutritious tree fruits readily available to foragers, with 14 g of protein in 100 g of fruit and high levels of iron and vitamin C. The fruit, which appears to be a small berry, is a drupe with a hard pit surrounded by a leathery outer layer. The outer layer is sweet and can be directly scraped off the hard pit, but this would not be a very efficient foraging strategy. Although fruits can technically be consumed raw and unprocessed, the hard inner pit makes it challenging to consume them in this manner. More typically, fruits are mashed in a mortar and pestle or ground in a food processor. Processed fruits can be used in a variety of ways. A product similar to almond milk can be prepared by finely mincing raw fruits and blending them with water. The mixture is then strained to collect the milk. Ground fruits can be packed into patties and used similarly to granola bars for longer-term preservation.

QUICK REFERENCE:

USES: edible
FORAGE SEASON(S): fall, winter
FORAGE PART(S): fruit
SPECIAL CONCERNS: none

FIREWEED

Chamaenerion angustifolium

PLANT: Herbaceous perennial, from 0.5–2.5 m in height, often growing in large colonies due to horizontally spreading rhizomes. Stems are mostly unbranched, typically reddish, and often hairy in the upper portion.

LEAVES: Leaves are spirally arranged, 5–20 cm long, and linear-lanceolate in shape. The secondary veins diverge at nearly a 90° angle from the main leaf vein. The tips of the secondary veins converge, forming a single, continuous vein around the edge of the leaf.

FLOWERS: Borne in erect racemes, from 5–50 cm in length. Individual flowers are nodding in the bud stage and becoming erect upon opening. Individual flowers are about 2.5 cm in width and are comprised of four paddle-shaped, pinkish-purple petals and four smaller, darker sepals. Eight long, pinkish-white stamens surround a long, white style, with the tip dividing into four curled stigmas.

FRUITS: A 4- to 10-cm-long upright capsule, becoming reddish when the seeds ripen. The capsule splits open at the tip, reminiscent of a peeled banana. Seeds are tiny (~1 mm long), brown, and have a tuft of silky hairs to aid dispersal.

ROOTS: The root system is fibrous and strongly rhizomatous, primarily occurring within 8 cm of the ground surface.

DISTRIBUTION AND HABITAT

Fireweed can be found throughout Canada, the northern and western portions of the United States, and at higher elevations of the Appalachians. It is typically found in open areas with moist soils, such as woodland edges, forest clearings, and along bodies of water. It is one of the first species to colonize recently burned forests, hence the common name.

FORAGING

Fireweed is probably best known as a forage flower, sometimes mixed with teas but more often used to make jelly, which uses a 2:1 ratio of flowers to water. After steeping flowers in boiling water, adding an acid, like lemon juice, will recover the beautiful, bright pink color lost during the steeping process. The young shoots, greens, and flowers of Fireweed can be mixed into salad greens. Stems can be lightly peeled and prepared like asparagus.

Little published pharmacological data supports the wide range of medicinal claims attributed to Fireweed; however, it can be safely used internally or externally.

QUICK REFERENCE:

USES: edible, medicinal
FORAGE SEASON(S): spring, summer
FORAGE PART(S): stems, leaves, flowers
SPECIAL CONCERNS: none

CHENOPODIUM
WILD QUINOA
GOOSEFOOT
LAMB'S QUARTERS

Chenopodium **spp.**

PLANT: Herbaceous, often weedy annuals and perennials (rarely shrub-like) with either an upright or prostrate (grows flat on the ground) growth form. The young leaves and stems of many species are farinose—appear powdery or mealy—due to the presence of small, white vesicular (inflated) hairs.

LEAVES: Leaves are alternately arranged, with leaf shapes varying amongst the various species. Most are either linear, ovate, or triangular, often with a flattened base. Leaf margins are often lobed or dentate but can be entire.

FLOWERS: Terminal or axillary spikes or panicles of glomerules (ball-shaped clusters of flowers). Flowers may be unisexual or bisexual. If unisexual, the terminal bud is typically male, while the remaining flowers are female. The perianth (sepals and petals) is five-parted and contains five stamens or two stigmas.

FRUITS: Fruits are achenes or utricles (dry, one-seeded fruit with a thin, membranous covering), usually enclosed within the collapsed perianth. Seeds are mostly horizontally oriented with a lenticular or globular shape and colored black, brown, or reddish brown.

ROOTS: Most species have fibrous roots that emanate from a short, branched taproot.

DISTRIBUTION AND HABITAT

Worldwide, there are over 100 species of *Chenopodium*. 34 species are found in North America, many of which are non-native. Some of these species are distributed throughout North America, while others have a more restricted range. They are often found in disturbed areas, such as trails, roadsides, and shorelines, especially the weedy and non-native species. However, some of the native species are found in more specific habitats.

FORAGING

Cultivated *Chenopodium*, Quinoa, is a widely grown pseudocereal (non-grasses whose seeds are used like grains) crop throughout large parts of South America. Quinoa gained popularity in North America and Europe in the early 2000s, primarily due to the seeds' high protein content and the crop's general adaptability to different growing conditions. The weedy wild relatives of cultivated *Chenopodium* share similar nutrition profiles and can be found in abundance, and are relatively easy to identify, at least to the genus. *Amaranthus* species may be look-alikes, but there are no concerning poisonous look-alikes. New leaves and tender shoots can be harvested in the spring and early summer. Leaves, sometimes called wild spinach, are boiled for 3–5 minutes and seasoned to taste. By mid-summer and late summer, leaves will take on a bitter flavor and are considered inedible by most, although not toxic. Seeds can be harvested in late fall by stripping seed heads into a collection container. Seeds can be quickly collected but separating the chaff from the seeds is very time-consuming. Several rounds of winnowing and rubbing seeds are required to remove the debris. The seeds also contain saponins (compounds that appear soap-like) that impart a bitter taste and cause digestive disturbance. Seeds should be soaked overnight and rinsed multiple times before drying for storage. You can also directly sprout seeds after soaking and eat the nutritious sprouts. This plant should be eaten in moderation.

CHICORY

Cichorium intybus

PLANT: Perennial herbaceous plants, often flowering in the first year and sometimes becoming somewhat woody, reaching up to 2 m in height. Stems are smooth but tough, green to purplish, and contain a milky sap. Branches are widely spreading at approximately 45° angles.

LEAVES: Leaves are alternate in arrangement and usually roughly hairy on the upper and lower surfaces. Leaves are up to 25 cm long and 7 cm wide, with their bases clasping the stem. The lower leaves are the largest and reminiscent of dandelion leaves—oblanceolate in shape, with several teeth or clefts along the margin. Leaves gradually become smaller and lose the teeth or clefts as you move up the stem.

FLOWERS: Flowers are borne in panicles or spike-like groups along and near the ends of the stems. Flowers are of the composite type, up to 2 inches across. Each flower is composed of numerous (usually 17) strap-shaped petals (ray flowers) with a blunt tip that has five teeth. They are primarily colored sky blue, but some individuals will have white or pinkish petals. There is a blue stamen at the base of each petal with darker blue anthers and a forked, blue and white style. Flowers are only open for one day, opening in the morning and closing later in the day.

FRUITS: Fruits are achenes, typically tannish to dark brown with darker mottling, up to 3 mm in length. They are oblong or thorn-like in shape with angled edges and blunt ends and are usually slightly curved. The wider end of the seed has a fringe of very short, white hairs.

ROOTS: Chicory has a long, fleshy taproot.

DISTRIBUTION AND HABITAT

Chicory can be found throughout most of North America, from southern Canada to Mexico. It tends to be found in disturbed sites, fields, and roadways.

FORAGING

Although the entire plant is safe to consume, Chicory's most well-known forage use is as a coffee substitute. Chicory has been used as a filler or substitute for coffee for hundreds of years. Historically, it was used when access to real coffee was restricted due to economic hardship or politics. In New Orleans, Chicory coffee is a popular tourist drink due to its earlier use as a coffee replacement during the Civil War when the Union navy blockaded the shipping ports in Louisiana, restricting access to coffee. To make Chicory coffee, collect roots in fall, wash thoroughly, dice, and roast until brown. After the roasted Chicory has cooled, use a coffee grinder to prepare a product ready for your coffee maker of choice.

QUICK REFERENCE:

USES: edible
FORAGE SEASON(S): fall
FORAGE PART(S): roots
SPECIAL CONCERNS: none

MINER'S LETTUCE
WINTER PURSLANE

Claytonia perfoliata (Synonym: *Montia perfoliate*)

PLANT: A fleshy winter or spring annual plant, anywhere from 1–50 cm in height.

LEAVES: The plant initially forms a rosette of erect basal leaves on 1–30 cm long pedicels. These leaves are up to 7 cm long and are broadly heart- to kidney-shaped. There is a pair of round, perfoliate leaves on flowering stems, giving the appearance of one circular leaf up to 10 cm in diameter.

FLOWERS: Above the perfoliate leaves emerges a cluster of 5–40 pink or white flowers. The flowers are five-parted and 3–10 mm wide.

FRUITS: The fruits are tiny 3-chambered capsules that contain up to three shiny, smooth seeds up to 5 mm long. The seeds are dispersed via ballistic dehiscence (forceful ejection of seeds from fruit).

ROOTS: This species has a fibrous root system.

DISTRIBUTION AND HABITAT

Miner's Lettuce is primarily found in North America's western coastal and mountainous areas, from British Columbia to Guatemala. Scattered occurrences east of the Rocky Mountains likely represent escapees from cultivation. It is primarily found in moist, shady habitats, such as creeks and near springs.

FORAGING

The California Goldrush peaked between 1848–1852 and brought hundreds of thousands of people to California. Food scarcity, especially fresh food, led to scurvy and other health problems for the miners and their families. Miner's Lettuce, so called because it was locally available and a great source of vitamin C for the deprived miners, became a highly sought-after forage greens and remains so today. Some gourmands claim Miner's Lettuce to be among the tastiest of all fresh greens. It is also among the few North American natives introduced to Europe and used extensively. Leaves can be eaten fresh or blanched, but most foragers find the fresh greens most appealing.

> **QUICK REFERENCE:**
>
> **USES:** edible
> **FORAGE SEASON(S):** spring, winter
> **FORAGE PART(S):** leaves, stems, flowers
> **SPECIAL CONCERNS:** none

SWEET FERN

Comptonia peregrina

PLANT: Small, woody shrub, up to 1.5 m in height. Stems are hairy to varying degrees, and the bark is grayish to brownish. They tend to form large colonies over time due to rhizomatous spreading.

LEAVES: Leaves are alternate in arrangement and lance-linear to oblong in shape, on short petioles or appearing stalkless. They can get up to 13 cm long and 2 cm wide. The leaf margins are pinnately lobed about halfway to the main vein, giving them a fern-like appearance. The upper leaf surface is dark green, and the lower surface is pale green. Both leaf surfaces are dotted with yellow glands and are usually hairy. They are also very sweetly aromatic and can be detected from a distance on warm days.

FLOWERS: Plants are monoecious, occasionally dioecious. Male flowers are in clusters of drooping catkins up to 5 cm long at the tips of one-year-old branches. Female flowers are in erect, globose catkins up to 5 mm long, from lateral buds below the male catkins. In dioecious plants, they are also formed at the branch tips.

FRUITS: Fruits are 8–15 egg-shaped nutlets up to 5 mm long that are contained within a cluster of bur-like bracts up to 2 cm across.

ROOTS: A rhizomatous spreading root system, which can result in the formation of dense thickets of plants.

DISTRIBUTION AND HABITAT

Sweet Fern is found in eastern North America, from North Carolina to southern Ontario to Nova Scotia. They are usually found in dry, sandy, or rocky soils in habitats such as pine barrens, forest clearings, and edges.

FORAGING

Sweet Fern is a good forage option for beginners because it is easy to identify based on its aromatic, fern-like leaves. It often grows near other easily identifiable forage foods, like blueberries. Leaves can be used to prepare a smooth tea, and seeds can be harvested and used as a seasoning. Tea can be prepared from fresh or dried leaves: approximately one tablespoon of finely chopped fresh leaves or a teaspoon of ground dried leaves per cup, steeped for 3–5 minutes. Seeds should be removed from the bur and can be used whole or ground into a powder; season to taste.

QUICK REFERENCE:

USES: edible
FORAGE SEASON(S): spring, summer, fall
FORAGE PART(S): leaves, seeds
SPECIAL CONCERNS: none

HAZELNUT
FILBERT

Corylus spp.

PLANT: Deciduous shrubs and small trees up to 15 m in height. Most species have deliquescent branching, meaning the trunk branches multiple times, leaving no central trunk. Most species are hairy to varying degrees, often glandular-hairy, primarily on stems and lower leaf surfaces.

LEAVES: Leaves are simple and roundish in shape, with doubly serrated margins.

FLOWERS: Individual plants are typically monoecious, although it is not uncommon to find individual plants with only male or female flowers present. Male flowers are catkins, growing in clusters on first-year growth and formed during the year before flowering. Female flowers are found on the same stems, usually distal to the male flowers. Female flowers have reduced parts and resemble buds with styles emerging from them. Both male and female flowers open very early in spring, before the leaves.

FRUITS: Fruits are roundish-shaped nuts that are often slightly laterally compressed and have noticeable ribbing on the outer surface. Fruits are contained in large, leaf-like bracts that are usually hairy and spiny, usually in clusters of several fruits.

ROOTS: Large root systems are formed, capable of spreading 4–5 m beyond the canopy.

DISTRIBUTION AND HABITAT

Corylus spp. are common in Southern Canada, the eastern half of the U.S., and the West Coast of the U.S. They are less common in the Great Plains/Great Basin and Gulf Coast areas of the U.S. There are two native species and at least four non-native species that can be found in the U.S. The two native species are found in open woods, thickets, riverbanks, savannas, and prairies, usually in dry to mesic soils.

FORAGING

The Hazelnut is a perfect forage food. It is easy to identify, has no poisonous look-alikes, and is easy to harvest. The biggest challenge with the Hazelnut harvest is gathering before the chipmunks or pests, such as the Hazelnut worm. Hazelnuts are contained in rough bracts that feel a bit like sandpaper when you pull them off the branches. You can harvest Hazelnuts as soon as you can easily remove the nut from the bract. They are still too green if the bract sticks firmly to the top of the nut; however, *slightly* green Hazelnuts will ripen post-harvest. Nut clusters can be pulled from the tree in their entirety, so harvest is fast and easy. After harvest, bracts should be removed and nuts spread out to dry for about two weeks. After drying, raw, in-shell nuts can be stored for a year or more in the refrigerator and 3–4 months in a cool, dry location. Nuts can be consumed raw, but most people prefer roasted Hazelnuts. You can roast Hazelnuts in the shell or with the shell removed. It is a bit easier to determine if your nuts are fully roasted if you remove the shells, but it is a personal preference. The suggested roasting temperature is 350° F for 10–15 minutes.

QUICK REFERENCE:

USES: edible

FORAGE SEASON(S): late summer to fall

FORAGE PART(S): fruits

SPECIAL CONCERNS: none

COMMON EUROPEAN HAZELNUT

Corylus avellana

KEY FEATURES

The Common European Hazelnut is a deciduous shrub native to Europe and Asia. It grows much larger than *C. americana* or *C. cornuta*. The nut of *C. avellana* is not completely covered by the involucre as it is in the other *Corylus* species but otherwise has very similar characteristics to *C. americana*. It is widely grown as an ornamental in North America.

AMERICAN HAZELNUT

Corylus americana

KEY FEATURES

American Hazelnut is a deciduous shrub native to North America. The involucre length on the mature nut of *C. americana* is up to 3 cm, and twigs are covered with glandular hairs.

BEAKED HAZELNUT

Corylus cornuta

KEY FEATURES

Beaked Hazelnut is a deciduous shrub native to North America. It can be distinguished from other *Corylus* species by the long involucre or "beak" covering the mature fruit, reaching up to 7 cm in length. It is further distinguished from *C. americana* by lacking glandular hairs on the twigs.

HAWTHORN
THORNAPPLE
QUICKTHORN

Crataegus spp.

PLANT: A group of shrubs and trees that reach up to 12 m in height. Twigs are thorny, with thorns reaching up to 10 cm long in some species, but more commonly, 1–6 cm. Some species also have abundant, compound thorns growing on the trunk.

LEAVES: On long shoots, leaves are spirally arranged. On short shoots, they are found in clusters. Leaf shape is variable amongst the species, but is generally elliptical to ovate, often deeply incised, and has serrated margins. Leaf venation is craspedodromous in most species, meaning the secondary veins terminate at the leaf margin, usually at the tip of the teeth.

FLOWERS: Borne in clusters of 1–50 flowers at the tips of short shoots. Flowers are five-parted, up to 3 cm wide, with mostly round-shaped petals (elliptical in some species) that are typically white but may be creamy or pale pink in a few species. Flowers are perfect, with 5–20 stamens (up to 45 in one species) shorter than the petals and 1–5 styles. Most species have a short flowering period, typically 7–10 days.

FRUITS: Round or oval-shaped pomes, up to 25 mm in diameter. Depending on the species, the color of ripe fruit may be yellow, red, purple, or black. Fruits often have persistent floral structures, such as the sepals and styles.

ROOTS: Root systems are variable between the species, with many having relatively shallow root systems, while other species may develop a deep taproot.

DISTRIBUTION AND HABITAT

Hawthorns can be found throughout the world. More than 100 species are broadly distributed throughout North America but seemingly absent from southern Florida and the Caribbean Islands. Most species are found in areas with mesic soils across a wide range of habitats.

FORAGING

Hawthorn has magical folklore and a long history of use in traditional medicine worldwide. Perhaps best known is that of Celtic tradition, where the Hawthorn tree was known as the "fairy tree" and believed to serve as a home for fairies and a portal to the fairy realm. Traditional medicine practitioners worldwide used (and still use) Hawthorn to treat heart ailments. Hawthorn tea is also sometimes recommended in times of emotional heartbreak and grief.

It can be difficult to identify this genus to the species level. Fortunately, all Hawthorns can be foraged, despite having some differences in flavor, texture, and size. In all cases, seeds should not be eaten. Like apple seeds, they are cyanogenic, and eating many seeds could be toxic. Young leaves can be harvested in early spring and used in fresh salads. Hawthorn fruit, or "haws," should be harvested in mid to late fall and can be used in various ways. For the first-time user, it is convenient to consider using haws in the same way you might use rose hips. Haws can be eaten raw, but each species and variety has a different flavor profile, and some species are more suited to raw consumption than others, so some aspects of Hawthorn forage may be trial and error. The making of jelly, tea, fruit leathers, and syrups are the most common ways to use Hawthorn haws.

QUICK REFERENCE:

USES: edible, medicinal

FORAGE SEASON(S): spring, fall

FORAGE PART(S): young leaves, fruit

SPECIAL CONCERNS: Large, sharp thorns may be present on stems. Hawthorn seeds should be avoided.

SCOTCH BROOM

Cytisus scoparius

PLANT: A deciduous shrub in the Pea family that usually has a dense mass of erect stems. The stems are strongly five-angled in cross-section and remain green year-round.

LEAVES: It has alternate compound leaves with three ovate leaflets. The leaflets are small (12 mm) and covered by short, appressed hairs. Due to the small size of the leaves, at a casual glance, the plant may appear leafless.

FLOWERS: Flowers are yellow and pea-like, approximately 2 cm long and 30 mm wide.

They are borne singly or in pairs from the leaf axils of the upper parts of the stem.

FRUITS: The fruit is a brownish-black flattened pod up to 5 cm long. The pod has long hairs on its seams and contains several seeds. When ripe, the pod rapidly splits open, often audibly, ejecting the seeds away from the parent plant.

ROOTS: The root system consists of a deep taproot with widely spreading lateral roots.

DISTRIBUTION AND HABITAT

It is native to Europe but has been widely planted as an ornamental in many places world-wide and is considered invasive in several areas. In North America, it is most prevalent in the coastal United States and Canada. Seedlings and young plants are sensitive to freezing temperatures, which largely keeps it from becoming established further inland. It naturally grows in dry, sandy soils in full sun. In North America, it is commonly found in dry, open, disturbed types of habitats, such as fields and pastures, along roadsides and railroads, in powerline rights-of-way, and recently logged areas.

FORAGING

Scotch Broom is an invasive species introduced to North America in the mid-19th century as an ornamental and quickly spread throughout North America's east and west coasts. It displaces native flora and creates a serious fire hazard. Scotch Broom was originally used to create handcrafted brooms and other handiwork. Brooms are one of the earliest human tools, with local flora and traditions shaping how brooms were made and used regionally. Scotch Broom was most likely used to create a crude broom for sweeping outdoor areas and walkways. Other species would have been used to create more refined brooms for dusting and cleaning. Although we may no longer have the knowledge or need to pro-duce our own brooms, the long, thin branches make Scotch Broom an excellent option for weaving and other handmade crafts. Due to its highly invasive categorization and detrimental environmental impacts, foraging and crafting with Scotch Broom is a great option for both new and seasoned foragers, and an opportunity to experiment with forage uses beyond food and medicine.

QUICK REFERENCE:

USES: crafting

FORAGE SEASON(S): any

FORAGE PART(S): stems

SPECIAL CONCERNS: Plant material is toxic and should not be consumed.

PERSIMMON
EBONY

Diospyros spp.

PLANT: A large group of shrubs and trees, many of which are ecologically and economically important species. They are noted for having hard, dense wood that can be darkly colored.

LEAVES: Leaves are alternate in arrangement and may be deciduous or evergreen. Leaf shapes range from lanceolate to elliptical to ovate, and most species have entire margins. The leaves are slightly thickened and have a leathery feel (coriaceous).

FLOWERS: With few exceptions, *Diospyros* is dioecious. Male flowers are borne in 2–15 flowered cymes, while female flowers are mostly solitary. Flowers are bell or urn-shaped with four lobes, usually curled back, and have a pleasant fragrance. Male flowers typically have 16 stamens, while female flowers have eight sterile stamens and four styles. Flower colors range from yellowish white to pale orange to orangish pink.

FRUITS: A fibrous or fleshy berry usually between 2 and 10 cm in diameter. Ripe fruit color varies among species and may be yellow, orange, red, purple, brown, or black.

ROOTS: Large root systems are formed, usually as wide as the tree's canopy.

DISTRIBUTION AND HABITAT

There are probably at least 700 species of *Diospyros* worldwide, mostly found in tropical regions around the globe. The actual number is difficult to determine, as this is a taxonomically challenging genus. In North America, up to 30 species may be found, most of which are only located south of the U.S.-Mexico border and several of which are non-native. Two species are native to the United States, one of which is only found in Texas (*D. texana*). The other species, *D. virginiana*, is found throughout most of the eastern half of the U.S., naturally occurring about as far north as New York City and central Illinois. However, it has been successfully grown as far north as southern Wisconsin and Michigan. The various species occupy a broad range of habitats. Many of the species are components of tropical forests. The U.S. native species are typically found in bottomland forests and abandoned agricultural lands.

FORAGING

Persimmon is an easy-to-identify, delicious fruit available to harvest even in the early winter months. Some foragers recommend harvesting after the first frost. Persimmon fruit should be very soft with wrinkly skin before it is harvested; unripe fruit is unpalatable. Fruit can be eaten raw, or the pulp can be processed in various ways, or even frozen for later use. Seeds should not be consumed.

QUICK REFERENCE:

USES: edible

FORAGE SEASON(S): fall, winter

FORAGE PART(S): fruits

SPECIAL CONCERNS: Seeds should not be consumed.

AUTUMN OLIVE

Elaeagnus umbellata

PLANT: Clonal shrub or small tree, up to 12 m in height. Mature specimens typically have dense, ascending branches, forming a crown as wide as it is tall. New branches are covered with white and brown scales and occasionally thorns. Older branches lose the thorns, become less scaly, and become an overall reddish-brown color.

LEAVES: Leaves are alternate in arrangement and elliptical to ovate, up to 8 cm long and 2.5 cm wide, on short (1 cm) petioles. Leaf margins are entire and often undulate. New leaves are covered by dense white scales on both surfaces. The upper surface becomes a glossy green with tiny white dots as they age. The lower leaf surface remains silvery-scaly, with both white and brown scales.

FLOWERS: Flowers are fragrant and are found in dense clusters of 3–10 flowers in the leaf axils of first-year stems. Individual flowers are funnel-shaped, about 1.5 cm long, with four triangular, cream-colored petals, yellowing with age. The flower stalks and sepals are covered with white scales.

FRUITS: An ovular, fleshy, and juicy drupe, up to 1 cm long, that is densely scaly when young. As it ripens, it becomes less scaly, turning pink or red when fully ripe.

Ripe fruits are sweet, each containing a single seed.

ROOTS: Deep, multi-branched root system.

DISTRIBUTION AND HABITAT

Native to Southern Europe and Central and Western Asia, it now occurs throughout most of North America. It is found in nearly every U.S. state, in Canada's southern mainland provinces, and as very scattered individuals in Mexico. It can be found in a wide variety of habitats because it was widely planted, for multiple reasons, throughout North America. It prefers habitats that are at least somewhat damp, such as along streams and rivers. It can form dense thickets in such sites and become the dominant species. It is considered a noxious weed and invasive in many locations in North America.

FORAGING

Autumn Olive is an excellent forage option because it is easy to identify and an invasive species found throughout much of North America. Fruits ripen to a reddish color in late fall and are easily harvested by shaking the heavily laden branches directly into a bucket. The fruits are nutritious and high in lycopene, the pigment responsible for the red color of tomatoes and a known antioxidant. The fruit has a sweet-tart taste and can be used like other harvestable fruits in baking, processed for dried fruit leather, preserved in jams, or frozen for future use.

QUICK REFERENCE:

USES: edible

FORAGE SEASON(S): fall

FORAGE PART(S): fruit

SPECIAL CONCERNS: Several shrubs and small trees produce red berries in the fall that could be confused with Autumn Olive. Some of these potential look-alikes are poisonous, such as several *Lonicera* species. Autumn Olive has uniquely speckled berries that help distinguish it from other similar species, but great care should be taken to ensure proper identification before consumption.

HUCKLEBERRY
DANGLEBERRY

Gaylussacia **spp.**

PLANT: Deciduous shrubs or subshrubs, up to 2 m in height.

LEAVES: Simple and alternate, obovate to oblanceolate in shape. They have reticulodromous leaf venation, meaning the secondary veins repeatedly branch and form a dense network of veins. Leaf margins are entire or crenate, sometimes revolute.

FLOWERS: Inflorescences are 2–8 flowered axillary or terminal racemes, occasionally with solitary flowers. They have five (sometimes four) petals fused nearly their entire length, resulting in an urn- or bell-shaped flower. Flower color ranges from greenish white to white to pink to orange to red, depending on the species. The flower has one style about as long as the petals and ten shorter stamens.

FRUITS: Fruits are globose, fleshy drupes with ten hard nutlets. Ripe fruit color is usually blue or black, occasionally white.

ROOTS: Roots are shallow and fibrous, typically less than 1 m below the surface.

DISTRIBUTION AND HABITAT

Ten species can be found in North America, all in the eastern half of the United States and adjacent parts of Canada. Most species are found in sandy soils of pine barrens and forests or acidic bogs.

FORAGING

Huckleberries are an excellent forage food for beginners. They are straightforward to identify with no poisonous look-alikes. The hardest part about Huckleberry forage is finding a good patch, with large, wild populations most likely distributed in specific habitats in rural, undisturbed locations. Michigan, Maine, and Canada still have commercial harvests from wild populations of Huckleberries. Huckleberries make excellent dried fruit, jams, jellies, and pies.

QUICK REFERENCE:

USES: edible
FORAGE SEASON(S): summer, fall
FORAGE PART(S): fruit
SPECIAL CONCERNS: none

QUICK REFERENCE:

USES: edible, medicinal
FORAGE SEASON(S): spring, summer, fall
FORAGE PART(S): leaves
SPECIAL CONCERNS: Do not harvest from chemically treated lawns.

CREEPING CHARLIE
GROUND IVY
GILL-OVER-THE-GROUND
ALEHOOF

Glechoma hederacea

PLANT: An herbaceous, perennial creeping plant in the Mint family. Individual stems can reach up to 50 cm in length.

LEAVES: Round to kidney-shaped, with scalloped edges, and opposite in arrangement. They can get up to 3 cm in diameter, on stalks up to 6 cm in length. Leaf nodes often have a fringe of white hairs, from which roots can develop and anchor the plant to the ground, allowing it to form dense mats.

FLOWERS: Flowers are bilaterally symmetrical and tubular and grow in clusters of 2–4 flowers from leaf axils in the upper parts of the stem. The petals are lip-shaped, with the upper lip notched, and the lower lip is three-lobed. The coloration ranges from light blue to purplish blue, with darker markings on the lower lip. Plants are gynodioecious, meaning a plant has either female flowers or flowers with both male and female structures (perfect).

FRUITS: Fruits are small, dark brown, egg-shaped nutlets.

ROOTS: The root system is shallow and fibrous.

DISTRIBUTION AND HABITAT

Native to Eurasia, ground ivy has been spread to many places worldwide. In North America, it is abundant in the eastern half and West Coast of the U.S. and Southern Canada. It is a common weed in lawns and forested areas where it is found. While preferring at least semi-shady habitats, it is not uncommon to see it growing in areas receiving full sun.

FORAGING

Creeping Charlie was an important part of the early European settler's apothecary. It was used liberally to treat many different ailments. Modern research suggests that teas prepared with dried leaves of Creeping Charlie will reduce mucous production and ease inflammation. Creeping Charlie leaves can also function in a manner similar to Hops and was used to clear ales before Hops were widely employed, which is reflected in the common name Alehoof. In addition to the once common medicinal applications, the stems and leaves of Creeping Charlie can be eaten raw or cooked like spinach.

JERUSALEM ARTICHOKE
SUNCHOKE

Helianthus tuberosus

PLANT: An herbaceous, hairy-stemmed perennial species of sunflower reaching up to 3 m in height. Despite the commonly used name of Jerusalem Artichoke, it is neither native to the Jerusalem area nor related to artichokes.

LEAVES: Leaves are opposite on the lower portion of the stem while often becoming alternate in the upper portion. The largest leaves are found in the lower part of the stem and can be up to 25 cm long and 15 cm wide, with a serrated to nearly entire margin. The leaves get smaller as you go up the stem. Leaf shape ranges from lanceolate to ovate, with a cuneate (wedge-shaped) base. Petioles can be up to 8 cm long and are usually winged. The lower leaf surface is hairy and gland-dotted, while the upper surface is coarse, giving it a sandpapery feel.

FLOWERS: Flowers are of the composite type (daisies, asters, etc.), borne at the top of the stem. A plant typically has 3–15 flowers on peduncles up to 15 cm long. Each flower is up to 9 cm across, with 10–20 yellow ray florets surrounding at least 60 yellowish-orange disc florets. The flowers have been reported to have a subtle, vanilla-like aroma.

FRUITS: The disc flowers eventually form a seed head comprised of dry, single-seeded fruits (cypselae) that are 5–7 mm long and bear two bristly scales on one end.

ROOTS: The root system is fibrous, with narrow, cord-like rhizomes that can grow over a meter in length. At the ends of the rhizomes, tubers form late in the year. The tubers are variable in size and shape, somewhat reminiscent of a ginger root, and are colored from white to tan to dark red.

DISTRIBUTION AND HABITAT

Jerusalem Artichoke is found primarily in the eastern half of the U.S. and southern Canada, with more widely scattered populations in the western half. It can be found in fields, riverbanks, woodland edges, thickets, roadsides, and waste areas, mostly in rich soils.

FORAGING

Jerusalem Artichoke tubers are best harvested after the first frost or even after several frosts. Harvesting after several frosts will help break down some of the less digestible carbohydrates and reduce the bloating and "windiness" that is often attributed to this delicious food when it is not harvested correctly. Tubers can be harvested like potato tubers. After washing, tubers can be eaten fresh or stored in a cool, dark place for several months or frozen for up to a year. Tubers can be prepared just like potato tubers, but roasting tubers produces a sweet, nutty delicious aroma.

QUICK REFERENCE:

USES: edible
FORAGE SEASON(S): fall, winter
FORAGE PART(S): rhizomes
SPECIAL CONCERNS: Harvest after frost.

QUICK REFERENCE:

USES: edible

FORAGE SEASON(S): spring, summer, fall

FORAGE PART(S): leaves, flowers, roots

SPECIAL CONCERNS: *Iris* species are toxic look-alikes, especially in early spring.

DAYLILY
DITCH LILY

Hemerocallis fulva

PLANT: An herbaceous, weedy perennial that rapidly grows in large clumps.

LEAVES: Basal leaves are long (up to 1 m) and narrow (~2 cm) with a floppy habit and sword-like shape.

FLOWERS: The common name "Daylily" references the large, orange, showy flowers (up to 20 cm across) that persist for only 24 hours. Flowers are arranged in panicles, with 3–6 flowers per stalk. Individual flowers are comprised of six tepals with six long stamens and a single style in the center.

FRUITS: Fruits are capsules, but *Hemerocallis fulva* is a sterile hybrid, so any apparent seeds would not be viable.

ROOTS: Extensive fibrous roots and thick, tuberous rhizomes support this species' ability to form large populations that exclude other species.

DISTRIBUTION AND HABITAT

Hemerocallis fulva is native to Asia but has broadly escaped cultivation and is distributed across North America. It is an invasive species in many parts of the United States and Canada. It is a long-lasting perennial with the ability to survive in many different environments and conditions. In North America, it often colonizes sunny disturbed areas, like ditches, embankments, and along railroad tracks.

FORAGING

Hemerocallis fulva is an introduced species that has become invasive in many parts of North America. It may be familiar to you as "Ditch Lily," commonly seen in spring and summer, where it has naturalized in large patches along roadsides and ditches. All parts of the Daylily are edible, either raw or cooked, but cooked is most recommended. As with all foraged foods, eating sparingly the first time you try it is recommended because some people have digestive concerns and experience a laxative effect after consuming large quantities. In the spring and summer, flower buds can be harvested. Battering flower buds and frying them is one of the many ways you can prepare these. In the fall and winter, tubers can be harvested and prepared like potato tubers. Like many forage foods, boiling with several water changes can help reduce bitterness, improve flavors, and reduce the likelihood of digestive disturbance.

HOLLY
INKBERRY
WINTERBERRY
YAUPON

Ilex **spp.**

PLANT: A group of trees, shrubs, and vines that may be evergreen or deciduous. The largest species attain heights of 25 m. Most species are noteworthy for their ability to regrow vigorously after pruning. Some species are used in landscaping and Christmas decorations due to their combination of glossy, dark green leaves and bright red berries. The branches are prominently covered with lenticels.

LEAVES: Leaves are simple and alternate, often thick and leathery with a glossy, dark green color, although some species have thin, papery non-glossy leaves. Leaf margins are usually entire or serrated, with some species having prominent marginal spines.

FLOWERS: *Ilex* are dioecious, having separate male and female plants, although occasionally, a plant will be monoecious.

Flowers are either solitary or borne in cymes. Flowers are generally inconspicuous, 0.3–1.5 cm in width, with flower color typically ranging from white to yellowish to greenish, although there are species with pink, red, or brown flowers. Flowers usually have 5–8 petals that are spreading to reflexed (straight out to bent back). Male plants tend to bear many more flowers than female plants.

FRUITS: Fruits are fleshy drupes, usually around 1 cm in diameter, with a thin, papery skin and 1–many hard seeds (pyrenes). The fruit color is red in most species, while in the other species, they are white, yellow, orange, or black.

ROOTS: Roots are composed of a sturdy, deep taproot—extending about 1 m below the surface—and fibrous lateral roots, growing primarily near the surface.

DISTRIBUTION AND HABITAT

There are well over 500 species of *Ilex* worldwide, with perhaps 40 species found in North America, although not all of those are native. In North America, they are found mostly in the eastern half of the U.S. and adjacent parts of Canada, Mexico, Central America, and the far western parts of the U.S. and Canada. The various species occupy a variety of habitats, usually in moist or well-drained soils that are at least slightly acidic.

FORAGING

Yaupon Holly (*Ilex vomitoria*) is the only plant found native to North America that contains caffeine and so makes a reasonable coffee substitute when prepared as a tea. Despite

the ominous-sounding scientific name, *Ilex vomitoria* will not cause vomiting unless consumed in a highly concentrated dose. Still, all forage foods should be cautiously used, especially the first time you try them. Several other *Ilex* spp. can be used to make tasty teas, including *I. cassine* and *I. verticillate*, but these do not contain caffeine. Tea leaves should be cured by drying; this can be accomplished by harvesting leaves and allowing them to air dry in the sun or roasting leaves in a 350° F oven. Like coffee beans, roasting time will influence the flavor of your tea. Use a half teaspoon of dried leaves per cup of tea, steeping for 3–5 minutes.

QUICK REFERENCE:

USES: edible

FORAGE SEASON(S): spring, summer, fall, winter

FORAGE PART(S): leaves

SPECIAL CONCERNS: Chinese Privet (*Ligustrum sinense*) is a poisonous look-alike.

JEWELWEED
TOUCH-ME-NOT

Impatiens capensis

PLANT: An herbaceous annual with smooth, succulent stems. It can reach up to 1.5 m in height and is often densely branched.

LEAVES: Leaves are alternate in arrangement, oval or oblong, with widely spaced teeth along the margins, usually around 6–8 teeth on each side of the leaf. Leaf length is up to 8 cm long. When submerged, the leaves appear silvery.

FLOWERS: Perfect flowers are borne in clusters of 1–3, in racemes on the upper parts of the plant. Individual flowers are approximately 1 cm long, tubular in shape, with a hooked nectar-filled spur at the rear of the flower. The flower's opening has three broad, circular, flaring lobes: two on the lower side and one on the upper. Flowers are orange in color, usually with many small red spots on the inner surface. The male and female floral structures mature at different times (dichogamous), with the anthers developing and dropping before the stigma is receptive. Additionally, small, inconspicuous flowers are sometimes produced near leaf bases. These cleistogamous flowers never open and are self-pollinating.

FRUITS: Fruits are a pod that can get up to 2.5 cm long. As the pod ripens, it inflates and builds up pressure. When fully ripe, the slightest touch causes the outer valves of the pod to coil up almost immediately, resulting in ballistic dispersal of the seeds within.

ROOTS: Roots are composed of a short tap-root with very shallow lateral branches.

DISTRIBUTION AND HABITAT

Jewelweed is most commonly found in moist soils, such as riverbanks and lakeshores, along the edges of springs, and wet wooded areas. While seemingly preferring shady locations, it is not uncommon to find them growing in areas with full sun. It is found mostly in the eastern half of the U.S. and the adjacent regions of Canada, and the Pacific Northwest, with much more scattered populations found in the Great Plains and Southern Rockies.

FORAGING

Most nature lovers and foragers first learn about the unique qualities of Jewelweed when they encounter stinging nettles, which is often found growing together with Jewelweed. Stinging Nettle irritation can be soothed with the juices of the Jewelweed stems. Crushing the stems with your hands and applying to the nettle-irritated locations does help reduce the burning discomfort. Jewelweed has also been suggested as a treatment for the pain associated with Poison Ivy and Poison Sumac (*Toxicodendron* spp.) exposure, but I have not found it particularly useful in this application. Leaves and stems are edible but must be boiled with at least two water changes.

QUICK REFERENCE:

USES: edible, medicinal
FORAGE SEASON(S): spring, summer
FORAGE PART(S): leaves, stems
SPECIAL CONCERNS: none

WILD POTATO VINE
MAN OF THE EARTH
MANROOT
WILD SWEET POTATO

Ipomoea pandurata

PLANT: An herbaceous perennial vine reaching up to 9 m in length. It is a vigorous grower in the right conditions and readily climbs up neighboring vegetation, often smothering it. In open areas, it sprawls along the ground. The stems are usually hairless and often have a reddish coloration.

LEAVES: Leaves are alternately arranged along the stem on long petioles and are heart-shaped, getting up to 15 cm long and 10 cm wide. Sometimes, smaller, ovate leaves are also produced.

FLOWERS: Flowers are borne in the leaf axils, in clusters of 1–5 flowers. They are funnel-shaped, with five shallow lobes up to 8 cm long and wide. The color is white, with the lower interior of the flower having a pink to purple color. Individual flowers are typically short-lived, opening in the morning and closing by mid-day or later under cloudy skies.

FRUITS: Fruit is a 2-celled capsule, with each cell containing 1–2 seeds. The seeds have a flattened appearance, with conspicuous hairs along the edges.

ROOTS: Plants form a large tuber that can be at least a meter deep. The tuber can get up to 75 cm long and 12 cm wide, attaining weights up to 10 kg.

DISTRIBUTION AND HABITAT

This species is found in the central and southern parts of the Midwest and the eastern United States. It is most common in disturbed areas, such as streambanks, woodland edges, thickets, roadsides, railways, and abandoned fields.

FORAGING

The Wild Potato Vine produces massive, edible roots. They are not reported to be the tastiest forage root, but what they lack in taste, they make up for in quantity. Roots should not be eaten raw. Peeling roots, cubing the tuber, and boiling for at least 30 minutes with a minimum of two water changes is the recommended method for processing.

QUICK REFERENCE:

USES: edible

FORAGE SEASON(S): spring, summer, fall, winter

FORAGE PART(S): roots

SPECIAL CONCERNS: Several species of *Ipomoea* are toxic, and care should be used to confirm ID before consumption.

WALNUT
BUTTERNUT

Juglans spp.

PLANT: A group of large deciduous shrubs and trees, ranging in height from 3 m to 50 m, characterized by a chambered pith (plant tissue in the center of the stem).

LEAVES: Alternate and pinnately compound, up to 5 cm long, containing 5–25 leaflets. Leaflets are sessile, or nearly so, with an oblong or lanceolate shape and usually a serrated leaf margin. Typically, all leaflets are the same size, with the terminal leaflet smaller in some species. Leaflets can be up to 15 cm long and 7 cm wide. In many species, the leaflets are aromatic and may be covered with glands, glandular hairs, or scales.

FLOWERS: Monoecious, with male flowers in the form of solitary catkins hanging from second-year branches. Male flowers form in late summer and persist through winter as a bud-like structure. Female flowers are found in terminal spikes or clusters of 2–25 buds on first-year branches.

FRUITS: A large nut surrounded by an adherent, fibrous husk. The outer surface of the nut is usually ridged but can be smooth. The seed within is fleshy and four-lobed and usually sweet-tasting.

ROOTS: They form very deep and wide root systems, often with a deep taproot. Roots secrete a chemical, juglone, that inhibits the growth of other plants.

DISTRIBUTION AND HABITAT

Worldwide, there are 21 *Juglans* species, six of which are present in North America. They have been widely cultivated and are adaptable to many habitats. Most species are found in creek and river floodplains, or other moist areas, such as near springs, although some are found in much drier habitats.

FORAGING

Juglans spp. are an accessible entry point for foraging. It is an easy group to identify with no poisonous look-alikes, and it can be found growing in sunny locations throughout hardiness zones 4–9 in North America. The nuts are encased in a yellow, tennis ball–like hull that has a warm, citrusy odor when rubbed. The fruits will begin falling from the trees in late summer and fall. You can harvest the fallen fruits and shake the tree limbs to bring down additional ripe fruits. To access the edible nut, first, remove the outer yellow hull. Removing the hull may require effort, but a straightforward method is to use your foot to scrape the hull on cement and pull off the remaining hull with your hands. If hulls are firmly attached, you can wait a few days for them to soften. After removing the hulls, the Walnuts should be spread out in a warm, dry location to dry for at least six weeks before attempting to remove the shell and access the edible meat. The North American Walnut has a much sturdier shell than the European species we are more familiar with in mixed nuts purchased from the grocery store. The standard nutcracker will not work on these nuts! A large rock or hammer can be used on the seam of the shell to break open the nut. Nut picks are handy tools for removing the meat.

QUICK REFERENCE:

USES: edible

FORAGE SEASON(S): late summer to late fall

FORAGE PART(S): fruit

SPECIAL CONCERNS: Wear gloves when working with walnuts to avoid dark stains on your skin.

BUTTERNUT

Juglans cinerea

KEY FEATURES

Butternut is a large, deciduous tree with pinnately compound leaves bearing 11–17 leaf-lets, including a terminal leaflet. The egg-shaped fruit is one of the best ways to distin-guish this species from *J. nigra*. Although both species are found in overlapping habitats, Butternut is less common because of significant losses due to Butternut Canker, a fungal disease caused by *Ophiognomonia clavigignenti-juglandacearum*.

EASTERN BLACK WALNUT

Juglans nigra

KEY FEATURES

Eastern Black Walnut is a large, deciduous tree with pinnately compound leaves bearing 15–19 leaflets with no terminal leaflet. Fruits are round and usually larger than the fruits found in *J. cinerea*.

WILD LETTUCE

Lactuca spp.

PLANT: *Lactuca* species are annual or biennial herbs that include the wild relatives of cultivated lettuce.

LEAVES: The leaves of most *Lactuca* species are dandelion-like, although not found in a basal rosette. Leaf shapes and margins are highly variable, even within a species and sometimes on a single plant. As the plant matures, leaves produce white, milky latex that causes a bitter taste.

FLOWERS: Dandelion-like flowers that range from yellow to sometimes orange are arranged on a loosely branched panicle. Flower size varies by species, but they are mostly small and not showy.

FRUITS: The fruit is a dry cypsela (single-seeded fruit), like a dandelion.

ROOTS: Roots are composed of a short taproot with shallow lateral branches.

DISTRIBUTION AND HABITAT

Over 100 *Lactuca* species are distributed worldwide, with the majority (at least 55) found in Asia and Europe. 12 species are broadly distributed across almost all of the United States and Southern Canada. Most species prefer warm, sunny locations with well-drained soil.

FORAGING

All *Lactuca* spp. found in North America can be foraged for fresh greens in the spring. A good rule is to avoid harvesting leaves with excessive white sap. Older leaves can be harvested and boiled as plants mature, but the taste will become increasingly bitter.

QUICK REFERENCE:

USES: edible
FORAGE SEASON(S): spring
FORAGE PART(S): leaves
SPECIAL CONCERNS: none

CANADA LETTUCE
FLORIDA BLUE LETTUCE
TALL LETTUCE

Lactuca
species of
interest

Lactuca canadensis

KEY FEATURES

Canada Lettuce is an herbaceous biennial with large, deeply lobed leaves.

PRICKLY LETTUCE
SCAROLE

Lactuca serriola

KEY FEATURES

Prickly Lettuce is the closest wild relative to cultivated *L. sativa* (lettuce that you would find in the grocery store). Like all North American *Lactuca*, Prickly Lettuce is an herbaceous annual or biennial; the leaves are highly variable but often pinnately lobed. Spiny leaf margins and edges distinguish this species from *L. canadensis*.

SWEETGUM
REDGUM

Liquidambar styraciflua

PLANT: A species of deciduous tree that reaches up to 41 m in height. Young twigs and branches often have corky wings. It gets its common name from the aromatic resin produced in the inner bark.

LEAVES: Leaves are alternate in arrangement and palmately lobed with five (occasionally three or seven) broad, pointed lobes, which gives them a star-shaped look. They are typically 8–13 cm long and wide, on a petiole of approximately the same length. When crushed, the leaves emit a resinous odor. This species is also known for its brilliant and showy fall colors.

FLOWERS: Individual trees are monoecious, with separate male and female flowers. Male flowers are produced in clusters on an erect raceme about 6 cm long. Individual flowers are greenish-yellow and small (3 mm), consisting of 4–8 stamens from a disc-shaped structure. Female flowers are on drooping stalks, bearing a globose cluster of small (3 mm) flowers, each consisting of 2 styles and 4–8 sterile stamens.

FRUITS: A hard, round compound fruit about 4 cm in diameter, consisting of 40–60 capsules. Each capsule contains 1–2 winged seeds, although it is common for many capsules to contain aborted seeds (seeds that didn't develop), which resemble sawdust. The outer surface of each capsule also bears two hard spikes, giving each fruit the appearance of a spiked ball.

ROOTS: Large root systems are formed, usually as wide as the tree's canopy.

DISTRIBUTION AND HABITAT

Sweetgum is native to the southern and eastern parts of the United States, roughly south and east of a line from New York City to Kansas City to San Antonio, as well as montane areas of southern Mexico and Central America. It is a popular landscape tree planted outside its native range. It is usually found naturally in areas with moist soil, such as lowland forests, seeps, and drier portions of swamps. It is shade-intolerant and usually only found in early successional forests. Eventually, more shade-tolerant species outcompete it.

FORAGING

Sweetgum produces a sweet, gummy latex that was used directly as chewing gum and as a chewing gum flavoring in the early 20th century. The gum can be scraped off areas of the Sweetgum bark that has been wounded. Leaf buds can be eaten raw in the spring. In the fall, seeds can be roasted, powdered, and used as a flour substitute or additive. Sweetgum also has several reported medicinal properties, including anti-bacterial and antifungal activity. It also contains the precursor to prescription antiviral medication, shikimic acid. Still, the commonly reported use of Sweetgum as an antiviral treatment is not supported by either documented traditional medicinal uses or any recent phytochemical research.

QUICK REFERENCE:

USES: edible, medicinal

FORAGE SEASON(S): spring, summer, fall

FORAGE PART(S): leaf buds, seeds, sap

SPECIAL CONCERNS: none

OLD WORLD CLIMBING FERN

Lygodium microphyllum

PLANT: A climbing or creeping fern with sporophytes up to 30 m in length. What appears to be the stem is the rachis of a single, freely branching frond. They grow vigorously throughout the year and quickly smother surrounding vegetation.

LEAVES: The fronds bear two types of leaflets, or pinnae, sterile and fertile. Sterile pinnae are unlobed and lanceolate in shape. Fertile pinnae are a similar overall shape but have a fringe of tiny inrolled lobes around the margin that cover sporangia (a fern's fruiting body).

FLOWERS: Ferns do not produce flowers.

FRUITS: Sporangia produce spores that develop small plants with sexual cells (gametophytes). The sexual cells unite and form a new sporophyte. The gametophytes are typically very small and inconspicuous.

ROOTS: Short, shallow roots are surrounded by wiry underground stems (rhizomes).

DISTRIBUTION AND HABITAT

It is native to tropical and subtropical areas of Africa, Asia, and Oceania. It has become established in the southern portions of Florida but is spreading northward. It is usually found in wet, disturbed sites, such as riverbanks, swamps, and hammocks.

FORAGING

While Old World Climbing Fern is not a traditionally recognized forage plant of North America, it has become one of the most destructive invaders of the past 30 years. It is currently estimated to cover more than two million acres of the south Florida habitat, including many ecosystems that support rare and endangered species. *Lygodium* spp. were brought to North America for ornamental purposes, but there are several reported traditional uses of *Lygodium* spp. found in their region of origin, including consumption of young fern fronds (though this is questionable and not recommended!), medicinal applications, and use as a crafting supply. In traditional southeast Asian basketweaving, *Lygodium* spp. were reported to be a primary material in basket weaving. To be used in weaving and binding, the rachis (stem) of the fern should be stripped of leaves, dried in the sun, and split into thinner strips. Other opportunities to use the fibers of this plant should be a thoroughly explored forage opportunity that benefits both the forager and the ecosystem by removing a tremendously damaging species from the environment.

QUICK REFERENCE:

USES: edible

FORAGE SEASON(S): late summer and fall

FORAGE PART(S): fruit

SPECIAL CONCERNS: Seeds are cyanogenic.

CRABAPPLE

Malus spp.

PLANT: Deciduous shrubs or trees, up to 20 m in height, with grayish to brownish platy or scaly bark. Twigs are often thorny and densely branched.

LEAVES: Leaf arrangement is alternate and varies from elliptical, ovate, oblong, or lanceolate in shape, with pinnate venation, up to 10 cm long. Leaf margins vary from lobed, dentate, serrate, or entire. The surface may be hairless or tomentose (densely covered by wooly, matted hairs), depending on the species.

FLOWERS: Flowers are borne in corymbs or panicles on the terminal ends of shoots, typically with 2–12 buds. Flowers are bisexual in all but one species and generally open when leaves emerge. Individual flowers have five roundish petals and can be up to 4 cm across. The color is white, pink or red. Flowers have 15–50 stamens that are often red and unequal in size, although they are usually shorter than the petals. The stamens surround 3–5 styles.

FRUITS: Fruit is an oblong or round drupe, up to 70 mm in diameter. The outer surface is hairless, smooth, and waxy, with the color ranging from green to yellow to red. The interior flesh is homogenous and encases 3–5 carpels at the center in a star-like arrangement, each of which bears 1–2 seeds. Seeds are somewhat teardrop-shaped, with a smooth surface and some shade of brown.

ROOTS: The root system is dense and fibrous, occupying about the same area as the crown.

DISTRIBUTION AND HABITAT

There are up to 55 species of *Malus*, ten of which are found in North America, with numerous cultivated varieties also present. They can be found throughout almost all of North America, seemingly absent from only the northernmost portions of Canada and Alaska. They occur in various habitats, such as meadows, forests, thickets, and wetlands.

FORAGING

All *Malus* species produce edible fruit, despite what you may have heard about Crabapples. These make a good forage option for people harvesting in urban areas as *Malus* frequently escape from cultivated landscapes. Crabapples are much more bitter and smaller than cultivated apple varieties, but they can be used in many recipes. They naturally contain large amounts of pectin, so jelly is an obvious use for Crabapple. Like all apple varieties, different Crabapples will have different flavor profiles and characteristics. As you become more experienced using Crabapples, you can use different types for different recipes. For example, more acidic-tasting varieties make better jellies, and more astringent-tasting varieties make better wines.

MALLOW

Malva spp.

PLANT: A group of herbaceous plants and shrubs that may be annual, biennial, or perennial, depending on the species. They may be upright or sprawling in growth form. Some species are considered weedy, while others are cultivated as ornamentals or food plants.

LEAVES: Leaves are alternate in arrangement. Leaf shape is variable amongst the species, but typically they are round to kidney-shaped, often palmately lobed, with crenate or dentate margins.

FLOWERS: Flowers are usually found in the leaf axils, either solitary or in fascicles (densely crowded cluster). Some species have flowers borne in terminal racemes. They are five-parted, up to 5 cm wide (depending on the species), and often showy. Color ranges from white to pink to purple, often with darker stripes.

FRUITS: Fruit is a schizocarp, a dry fruit that splits into single-seeded parts (mericarps). *Malva* spp. typically have round or wheel-like schizocarps that split into 6–20 wedge-shaped mericarps.

ROOTS: The roots are large taproots.

DISTRIBUTION AND HABITAT

At least 15 species of *Malva* can be found in North America, all non-native except for one species that is native only to the Channel Islands off the coast of Southern California (*Malva assurgentiflora*). Together, they are distributed throughout almost all of North America, scarce or absent only in the Caribbean Islands. While preferred habitats are variable amongst the species, they are typically found in disturbed, open habitats such as vacant lots, roadsides, and pastures.

FORAGING

The marshmallow we use for roasting on camping trips and in s'mores has its origins with the plants in the Mallow family. All Mallows contain a mucilaginous, sugary liquid in all plant parts, with the highest mucilage content found in the roots. All parts of the plant are edible, but the roots are most often foraged. You can prepare and use the roots in a variety of ways, but the most useful preparation method is powdering. To powder Mallow roots, harvest, clean, dice, dry, and process with a food processor to obtain a powder. The powder can be used as a thickening agent, tea, gelatin substitute for vegan recipes, and in a huge variety of healthcare and beauty products—you are limited only by your creativity in how you might use this valuable forage product.

QUICK REFERENCE:

USES: edible, medicinal
FORAGE SEASON(S): summer, fall, winter
FORAGE PART(S): roots
SPECIAL CONCERNS: none

MUSK MALLOW

Malva moschata

KEY FEATURES

Malva moschata is an herbaceous perennial with showy pink flowers with a distinctive musk scent. Musk Mallow is native to Europe but has escaped cultivation and can be found throughout most western and eastern North America.

CHEESES
COMMON MALLOW

Malva sylvestris

Key Features

Malva sylvestris is the "type species" for the *Malva* genus. It is an herbaceous perennial with showy, purple flowers. Like *M. moschata*, it is native to Europe and has escaped cultivation but has naturalized throughout North America.

QUICK REFERENCE:

USES: edible
FORAGE SEASON(S): early summer
FORAGE PART(S): fruit
SPECIAL CONCERNS: none

MULBERRY

Morus spp.

PLANT: A fast-growing deciduous shrub or tree with poisonous, milky sap. The genus contains many economically and ecologically important species. *Morus alba* leaves are the exclusive food of silkworms used to produce silk.

LEAVES: Leaves are alternately arranged and simple. They may be entire or deeply lobed, and leaf margins are toothed. Significant variability is present even within a single specimen.

FLOWERS: Most species are dioecious. Male flowers are spikes borne in the leaf axils. Female flowers are short spikes or dense clusters, usually sessile. Flowers are four-merous with a superior ovary.

FRUITS: Fruits are aggregate.

ROOTS: Roots are woody and usually as wide as the tree's canopy.

DISTRIBUTION AND HABITAT

There are 64 species of Morus distributed worldwide. Three species are found in North America, with one native, *M. rubra*, and two introduced, *M. alba* and *M. nigra*.

FORAGING

Morus spp. are a vastly underutilized forage crop that is easy to find, identify, and harvest. When ripe, Mulberry will easily come off the tree, so some foragers will speed up their harvest by spreading tarps under trees and shaking the branches to cause the ripe berries to fall from the trees. Berries can be eaten fresh, dried like raisins, or used like other berries for baking and preserves.

WHITE MULBERRY

Morus alba

KEY FEATURES

Morus alba is a deciduous shrub or tree that produces abundant edible berries in spring. It is distinguished from the other species found in North America by having white fruits that tend to be slightly less juicy and have a somewhat different flavor. White Mulberry is native to Asia.

RED MULBERRY

Morus rubra

KEY FEATURES

Morus rubra is a deciduous shrub or tree that produces abundant edible berries in the spring. It is distinguished from other *Morus* species found in North America by having reddish-purple to black fruits. *Morus rubra* is native to North America.

EVENING PRIMROSE

Oenothera biennis

PLANT: Herbaceous upright biennial, up to 2 m tall. It is typically covered with short, stiff hairs over most parts of the plant.

LEAVES: In the first year, leaves form a basal rosette; in the second year, leaves are present on the flowering stem. Leaves are lanceolate to elliptic, with bluntly toothed margins. Basal leaves tend to be larger (2 cm x 30 cm) than the stem leaves (1 cm x 20 cm).

FLOWERS: Borne at the tip of the stem and bloom successively from the bottom up. Typically a few to several open at a time, opening in the evening and closing during the day. Flowers can be up to 5 cm across, with four yellow, heart-shaped petals, eight yellow stamens, and a cross-shaped stigma. The four sepals are up to an inch long and are bent backward, pointing away from the flower.

FRUITS: Fruits are tube-shaped, slightly curved capsules, up to 4 cm long, with prominent hairs on the surface. The capsules have eight small lobes at the tip and contain irregularly shaped black seeds that average about 1.5 mm in length.

ROOTS: This species forms a deep, fleshy taproot.

DISTRIBUTION AND HABITAT

It is native to central/eastern North America but has been introduced and spread worldwide in temperate and subtropical regions. It is typically found in disturbed ground in open areas with dry, sandy soils.

FORAGING

Many people are aware of the medicinal properties attributed to Evening Primrose, including treatments for PMS, eczema, and diabetes, in addition to other claims. No peer-reviewed literature provides strong evidence to back the medicinal properties attributed to Evening Primrose. Fewer people are aware that Evening Primrose is a delectable forage plant. The large taproot of first-year plants can be harvested between fall and spring. Roots should be peeled and heated in boiling water for at least 20 minutes. Water should be changed twice during the boiling process to help eliminate bitterness and remove toxins that may otherwise cause stomach upset.

USES: edible, possibly medicinal

FORAGE SEASON(S): fall and spring

FORAGE PART(S): flowers, roots

SPECIAL CONCERNS: none

POKEWEED

Phytolacca americana

PLANT: An herbaceous perennial plant or shrub that can reach up to 7 m in height and nearly as wide. Stems are stout, smooth, and green and turn purplish near the end of the growing season. Individual plants may be single- or multi-stemmed. Stems are mostly upright during the first half of the growing season, after which the upper branches start spreading horizontally. They die back to the ground each winter.

LEAVES: Leaves are alternate, on 1–6 cm petioles, and are ovate to lanceolate in shape, with a roundish base and pointed tip. The margins are entire. They can get up to 40 cm long and 18 cm wide. The leaves have an unpleasant aroma when crushed.

FLOWERS: Flowers are borne in erect or drooping racemes up to 30 cm long, containing a few to 50+ flowers. The raceme is usually colored dark pink. Individual flowers are five-parted, lack petals, and have greenish-white or white sepals (occasionally pink or purplish) about 0.5 cm wide. There are usually ten stamens in a whorl.

FRUITS: Fruits are round berries formed from each flower. They start green, turn white, then ripen to a dark purple color. Inside the berry are shiny black lenticular seeds.

ROOTS: These plants develop deep taproots over time, with moderately spreading horizontal rootlets. The roots are tannish in color, with a white interior flesh. The root has annual growth rings, like a tree trunk.

DISTRIBUTION AND HABITAT

It is found primarily in the eastern half of the United States and Mexico, the west coastal area of the United States and Canada, and the far southern parts of Ontario and Quebec. It is infrequently found in the Great Plains and desert southwest part of the United States. There is evidence that it has been gradually spreading northward since European settlement. It tends to be found in a variety of disturbed areas, such as pastures, recently cleared woodlots, trails, and neglected areas.

FORAGING

Pokeweed is one of the most controversial of all forage plants. Although it is poisonous if not properly harvested and processed, it was and still is consumed, particularly by people in Appalachia and the southern United States. It was even available commercially canned until relatively recently. A traditional southern dish called "Poke Sallet" or "Poke Salad" is made from young, tender sprouts. It is generally advisable to harvest sprouts that are shorter than 10–20 cm, but this is a guideline and not a hard and fast rule. Harvested shoots should be very floppy and flexible. These are prepared by boiling with a minimum of two water changes (three is advised) for 30 minutes. After cooking, the greens are traditionally fried in bacon grease and seasoned with salt and molasses. Some older foragers report that in some parts of the country, Poke Salad was not as much a delicacy but a reflection of the ingenuity required of those experiencing impoverished conditions and food scarcity.

QUICK REFERENCE:

USES: edible

FORAGE SEASON(S): spring

FORAGE PART(S): young stems

SPECIAL CONCERNS: This plant should never be eaten raw; it must be harvested and processed properly to remove toxins.

SPRUCE

Picea spp.

PLANT: A group of evergreen conifers that usually develop a prominent conical or spire-like shape when fully grown, with a maximum height of around 60 m. Due to the peg-like needle bases (pulvini), the branches grow in whorls and are noticeably rough. They tend to have scaly bark that often has numerous resin blisters.

LEAVES: The needles are borne singly, spreading in all directions around the twig. They are usually stout with a sharply pointed tip, which leads to many species being noticeably prickly. A few species have more lax needles that can be grasped without the prickly feeling. The needles are mostly square in cross-section but may appear triangular or flattened, and they have 1–2 rows of resin canals that look like faint white stripes to the naked eye. Individual needles are shed after 4–10 years.

FLOWERS: Pollen and seed cones are formed on year-old twigs. Pollen cones are axillary and usually in groups. They are oblong and yellowish to purplish. Seed cones are typically formed in the upper branches, are oval to round in shape, and hang down from the twig.

FRUITS: Seed cones typically ripen at the end of one growing season, at which point they are shed. Occasionally, cones may remain on the tree for a few years. Mature seed cones have thin, fan-shaped scales and winged seeds within. Seedlings have 5–15 needle-like cotyledons (first leaves that appear when germinating).

ROOTS: Roots are woody and usually as wide as the tree's canopy.

DISTRIBUTION AND HABITAT

The Spruces are a characteristic tree of the Northern Temperate and Boreal regions. There are eight *Picea* species in North America, including one non-native species. They are well-distributed across the northern half of North America, with southward extensions at higher elevations down the West Coast, the Rocky Mountains, and the Appalachian Mountains. Due to their popularity as landscape trees, Spruces are commonly seen outside their natural ranges and habitats. In their native habitats, they experience cold, snowy winters, with some species preferring dry habitats while others are better adapted to wet soils.

FORAGING

Spruce tip foraging has become increasingly popular. It may be because foraging options are so limited in early spring in some areas that Spruce is a fun forage to experiment with, or it may be that more people just genuinely enjoy spruce tips. The young needles can be eaten fresh, used as a seasoning, prepared in an infusion, or used in beer brewing. Although most conifer tips can be forage food, use extreme caution to ensure you do not harvest from Yew (*Taxus*) species or other non-edible species.

QUICK REFERENCE:

USES: edible
FORAGE SEASON(S): late winter, spring
FORAGE PART(S): new growth tips
SPECIAL CONCERNS: Yew species are deadly poisonous look-alikes.

QUICK REFERENCE:

USES: edible
FORAGE SEASON(S): fall
FORAGE PART(S): needles, seeds
SPECIAL CONCERNS: none

PINE

Pinus spp.

PLANT: Evergreen coniferous shrubs (few) and trees, ranging in height from 15–80 m. When young, they tend to have a conical shape, maturing with a flat or round-topped crown. The mature bark is variously plated or scaly. Branches are in pseudo whorls, with short shoots and long shoots.

LEAVES: The leaves are dimorphic (two types). Needle-like leaves are born in fascicles from the short shoots. Depending on the species, there are 1–6 needles per fascicle. The needles are round or three-angled in cross-section. At the base of each fascicle are 12–15 overlapping scale-like leaves. These leaves are brownish and are not photosynthetic. Needles last any-where from 2–12 years before being shed, while scale leaves are usually never shed.

FLOWERS: Male and female flowers are separate on the same tree (monoecious). Pollen (male) cones are in dense, spike-like clusters at the base of the current year's growth and may be yellow, tan, red, blue, or purplish. Female cones are conical to cylindrical and may be erect or hanging. The cone scales are woody with a thick-ened tip. They mature in 2–3 years, with some species dependent on fire to open up the scales.

FRUITS: The seeds are found within the cones and may be winged or unwinged. Seedlings have 3–18 needle-like cot-yledons (first leaves that appear when germinating).

ROOTS: Roots are woody and extend far beyond the tree canopy.

DISTRIBUTION AND HABITAT

Pines are native to many areas of the Northern Hemisphere, with at least one species crossing the equator. There are 38 *Pinus* species in North America, including at least one well-established non-native species. Together, these 38 species are found throughout nearly all of North America. The various species naturally grow in a wide variety of habi-tats, from deserts to swamps, in both the coldest and hottest environments. They are also popular ornamental trees, with many species and cultivated varieties planted far outside their natural ranges and habitats.

FORAGING

The needles and seeds of most *Pinus* spp. are edible, but a few species should be avoided. Those to avoid contain a toxic compound called isocupressic acid. These species include Ponderosa Pine (*P. ponderosa*), Lodgepole Pine (*P. contorta*), and Monterey Pine (*P. radiata*). Traditionally, the needles of White Pine (*P. strobus*) were used in teas to prevent and treat scurvy and have other health benefits. Seeds can be obtained from nearly ripe cones in the fall. Store cones until seeds are released. Seeds can be roasted or consumed raw.

PLANTAGO
PLANTAIN

Plantago spp.

PLANT: Herbaceous annuals and perennials that are mostly stemless.

LEAVES: Leaves are alternate in arrangement and primarily basal, although they are opposite in the small number of species that have stems. Leaves are variable in shape but tend towards being ovate to elliptical, often with a fleshy composition, with 3–5 parallel veins. Margins may be entire or toothed.

FLOWERS: Flowers are tiny and inconspicuous, densely clustered on erect spikes up to 40 cm tall. They have 3–4 sepals and petals that are usually translucent to some degree and greenish to white in color. There are either 2 or 4 stamens surrounding an elongate stigma.

FRUITS: The fruits are capsules with a lid that separates from the top, called a pyxis. Each capsule contains anywhere from 1–35 dark brown or black seeds.

ROOTS: Root systems are typically fibrous and branching, occasionally with a taproot.

DISTRIBUTION AND HABITAT

There are around 210 species of *Plantago*, and they can be found on all continents except Antarctica. Some species have become cultivated around the world and have become cosmopolitan weeds. In North America, there are around 35 species, approximately 2/3 of which are native. As a whole, they can be found throughout nearly the entirety of North America. They occur in a variety of habitats, typically with moist soils, although there are some species adapted to dry conditions.

FORAGING

Plantago spp. are widespread, easy to identify, and available to harvest most of the year. In the spring and summer, young, fresh leaves can be gathered and blanched. Older leaves are less palatable but can be boiled longer to improve flavor. Seeds can be harvested in the fall and ground into flour.

The most common medicinal use of *Plantago* spp. is as a poultice to draw infection from wounds. To use as a poultice, fresh or dried plant material is macerated, and sufficient water is added to create a thick paste. The paste is applied to wounds or insect bites and covered—my Grandma would cover the paste with another clean plantain leaf. The poultice should be changed when the paste dries.

QUICK REFERENCE:

USES: edible, medicinal
FORAGE SEASON(S): spring, summer, fall
FORAGE PART(S): stems, leaves, seeds
SPECIAL CONCERNS: none

RIBWORT PLANTAIN
ENGLISH PLANTAIN

Plantago lanceolata

KEY FEATURES

A Eurasian native, it has become an established weed in many areas outside of its native range. In North America, it is found nearly throughout, especially concentrated across the eastern half of the U.S. and adjacent parts of Canada, as well as along the Pacific Coast, commonly found along roadsides, trails, and in urban areas, especially in disturbed sites. It is a rosette-forming perennial with leafless, hairy flower stalks. The leaves are lanceo-late in shape, with conspicuous parallel veins. The flower spikes can get up to nearly 1 m in height but, more commonly, are about half that. They are grayish to yellowish in color and noticeably shiny.

COMMON PLANTAIN
BROADLEAF PLANTAIN
GREATER PLANTAIN

Plantago
species of
interest

Plantago major

KEY FEATURES

A Eurasian native that has naturalized in many areas around the world. It is widely distributed throughout most of North America. It is a rosette-forming annual or perennial, with large ovate leaves up to 40 cm long and 20 cm wide. Flowering spikes can reach up to 0.5 m in height and are brownish or greenish in color.

MAYAPPLE
WILD MANDRAKE

Podophyllum peltatum

PLANT: An herbaceous perennial up to 40 cm tall. They are usually found growing in large colonies derived from a single rhizome.

LEAVES: Leaves are large, up to 40 cm wide, and are palmately lobed, with 5–9 lobes that may be deeply or shallowly cut. Often, each lobe itself is two-lobed. The leaves are typically held horizontally and are widely spreading, giving them an umbrella-like appearance. A single leaf is produced on nonflowering shoots, while flowering shoots have a pair of leaves.

FLOWERS: Flowers are solitary, on a nodding/drooping stalk that grows from where the two petioles diverge. A flowering stem will produce 1–8 flowers. Each flower is up to 6 cm across and radially symmetrical, with 6–9 white (occasionally pink) petals and twice as many stamens. Depending on latitude, they are typically in flower from late April to mid-May.

FRUITS: The fruit is a berry up to 6 cm in diameter. It ripens in late summer, with a yellowish color but may be orange or dark red. Within each fruit are 30–50 oval-shaped seeds about 6 mm long.

ROOTS: Mayapples have a creeping underground rhizome that can elongate up to 20 cm yearly. These rhizomes produce many stems.

DISTRIBUTION AND HABITAT

They are distributed across the eastern half of the United States, except the Florida peninsula, as well as southern Ontario, Quebec, and Nova Scotia. They are mostly found in rich deciduous forests.

FORAGING

Mayapple is another forage plant that is controversial regarding its safety as an edible forage food. All plant parts and unripe fruits are extremely toxic. But the completely ripened fruit is safe and edible. Fruits ripen in summer to late summer, and ripe fruit will be yellow, soft, mushy, and easily fall off the plant. Never eat fruit that feels firm or green. Mayapple is not a forage plant to be attempted by a novice forager and should only be harvested with an experienced guide. Pregnant people should not consume even ripened Mayapple fruit. Seeds should not be consumed in fresh fruit or processed fruit. Berries can be used in baking and preserves after seeds have been removed.

QUICK REFERENCE:

USES: edible (only ripe fruit)

FORAGE SEASON(S): late summer

FORAGE PART(S): fruit

SPECIAL CONCERNS: Unripe fruit contains the cytotoxin podophyllin, and consumption will cause severe gastrointestinal distress or potentially more serious poisoning.

CHOKECHERRY
BITTER BERRY
BIRD BERRY

Prunus virginiana

PLANT: An often-suckering shrub or small tree, up to 10 m in height (occasionally taller). The bark is typically gray or brownish gray with horizontal lenticels. Smooth when young, the bark becomes rougher and furrowed with age. Twigs can be reddish-brown to gray, usually smooth and hairless, but can be hairy in some individuals. Leaf buds are reddish-brown, with each bud scale having a paler edge.

LEAVES: Leaves are alternately arranged and simple, with an elliptic to ovate shape, usually the widest above the middle of the leaf. The leaf tip abruptly tapers to a sharp point. Leaf margins are finely serrated with pointed teeth. The upper surface is usually a dark, glossy green, while the lower surface is paler, sometimes with white or yellow hairs along the lateral veins. The petioles are up to ¾ of an inch long, with one or more glands near the leaf blade.

FLOWERS: Aromatic flowers are found in nodding or hanging racemes up to 15 cm long, bearing 20–60 flowers, originating from twigs' tips and lateral shoots. Flowering occurs after leaf emergence. Individual flowers are up to 1 cm across, with five circular white petals surrounding a yellowish center. Up to 25 stamens surround a single central style.

FRUITS: The fruit is a smooth, shiny round drupe, up to 15 mm in diameter, developing from each flower. The color ranges from red to dark purple to black. Within each fruit is a single, hard seed.

ROOTS: *Prunus* has a deep, rhizomatous root system that can extend well beyond the tree's canopy.

DISTRIBUTION AND HABITAT

Chokecherry is found throughout most of North America, from Alaska to Newfoundland, south to the U.S.-Mexico border. Primary habitats include open woodlands, forest edges, riverbanks, and roadsides.

FORAGING

Chokecherry was an important food for many First People in North America. It was harvested for juice and fruit leathers and used in pemmican—a mixture of pulverized dried meat, fat, and dried berries. Pemmican is made into cakes, used on long journeys, and stored as a high-calorie winter food source. Berries can be harvested in late summer; care should be taken to ensure berries have reached peak ripeness. Fruit should be dark magenta to nearly black and only slightly bitter. As the fruit matures, the bitter flavor dis-

sipates. After harvest, the fruit should be boiled and strained to remove the cyanogenic seeds. The prepared fruits can be used for jellies and fruit leathers. Chokecherry juice can be used to make wine and syrup.

QUICK REFERENCE:

USES: edible

FORAGE SEASON(S): late summer

FORAGE PART(S): fruit

SPECIAL CONCERNS: Chokecherry fruit seeds are cyanogenic and should not be consumed. *Rhamnus cathartica* is a poisonous look-alike. *Prunus* species all contain one seed per fruit; *Rhamnus* fruits contain multiple seeds. Identification should be confirmed with several sources before consumption.

WILD PLUM

Prunus americana

KEY FEATURES

Wild Plum is a deciduous shrub or small tree that is distributed throughout the United States. Trees typically do not exceed 6 m in height. Fruit from the Wild Plum can be eaten raw, but it is much smaller than the cultivated plum and contains a single large seed pit. Processing into preserves is preferred.

BLACK CHERRY

Prunus serotina

KEY FEATURES

Black Cherry is a large deciduous tree reaching up to 25 m in height. Black Cherry is native to eastern North America and Mexico and distributed throughout the United States. Fruits ripen in late summer and can be harvested when they are nearly black. Fruit can be eaten raw, but seeds should not be consumed. Harvested fruit can be used for juice, preserves, or dried fruit leathers. The bark and leaves of Black Cherry are often used in medicinal teas.

QUICK REFERENCE:

USES: edible, medicinal, crafting/fiber
FORAGE SEASON(S): spring, summer, fall
FORAGE PART(S): leaves, stems, roots
SPECIAL CONCERNS: Do not consume seeds.

KUDZU

Pueraria montana

PLANT: A perennial, semi-woody vine in the Pea family that grows exceptionally fast, up to 30 cm per day. Mature stems are dark brown, woody, and up to 10 cm in diameter. Plants climb using tendrils; stems can root at the nodes, forming secondary root crowns. Up to 30 stems can be produced from one root crown.

LEAVES: It has compound leaves that are alternate in arrangement. Each leaf consists of three broadly ovate leaflets, which are up to 20 cm long and wide and usually have three lobes.

FLOWERS: Flowers are borne in hanging racemes from the leaf axils and have a typical pea-flower appearance. They are usually purplish and up to 2 cm wide. They are pleasantly fragrant, many likening the smell to that of grapes.

FRUITS: Fruits are hairy, brown, flattened pods up to 13 cm in length. Each pod contains 3–10 seeds, with usually only 1–2 of them being viable.

ROOTS: Over time, Kudzu develops a very large semi-woody, tuberous taproot. They can get up to 2 m long and 0.5 m wide and attain a weight of up to 180 kg.

DISTRIBUTION AND HABITAT

A native of Asia, Kudzu was widely planted in the southern U.S. during the late 1800s and early 1900s for various reasons. It is now found in at least 30 U.S. states and one Canadian province (Ontario). It is most common in the southern states but has been reported as far north as Detroit, MI, and Boston, MA, and as far west as Dallas, TX, and southeast Nebraska, with isolated occurrences in Hawaii and Oregon. It tends to be found in open, disturbed areas, such as roadsides, powerline rights-of-way, and fallow fields. It thrives in areas that experience mild winters and hot, humid summers.

FORAGING

Kudzu is a destructive invasive species with a secret: it is edible and reasonably tasty. Young leaves and stems can be eaten fresh or blanched; flower buds are edible raw, and (reportedly) sweet. Starch can be obtained from the large, tuberous taproot. The process of extracting starch from the massive taproot is very labor intensive. Still, there is exciting progress by pioneering foragers who are beginning to see the value of the invasive vine. One pilot program engages a community of foragers in a week-long educational camp experience where foragers learn how to harvest and use Kudzu. These types of innovative, sustainable solutions represent the future of foraging.

Kudzu is a medicinal plant used in traditional Chinese medicine to treat heart disease, diabetes, and other disorders. Fibers from the vines are used to produce rope, cloth, and paper.

PEAR

Pyrus spp.

PLANT: A group of 1–many stemmed decid-uous trees and shrubs up to 30 m in height, with many widely cultivated species and varieties.

LEAVES: Leaves are alternate in arrange-ment, with the shape ranging from ellipti-cal to ovate to oblong, usually with a firm or leathery feel. Margins may be entire or serrated to some degree.

FLOWERS: Flowers are borne in terminal clusters of 4–9 flowers, opening before or during leaf-out. Flowers are radially symmetrical, with five white petals and 20 stamens.

FRUITS: The fruit is a pome that is globose to ovate in shape, if not the stereotypical pear-shape (pyriform). Ripe skin color is usually yellow, green, red, or brown, and often spotted, up to 12 cm in diameter. The flesh is white or creamy in color and con-tains abundant stone or grit cells, which give pears that gritty texture when eaten.

ROOTS: They typically have a shallow but dense, fibrous root system, occasionally producing suckers.

DISTRIBUTION AND HABITAT

There are at least five species in North America, all of which are non-native. They are mostly found in the eastern half of the U.S. and adjacent parts of Canada, with more scat-tered and isolated populations to the west. They are typically found in old pastures and fields, around old homesteads, in fencerows, or on woodland edges.

FORAGING

In the mid-1960s, someone determined that the North American landscape needed to be flooded with fruit trees that produced stinky flowers and poor-quality fruit growing on thorny branches. And so the Callery (Bradford, Aristocrat) Pear was introduced to North America. The Callery Pear is probably most known for its awful smell and simultaneously beautiful display of showy white flowers in early spring. Over the last decade, the tree's propensity to stink up the neighborhood and become an invasive species across much of North America has caused it to lose favor in the ornamental landscaping industry. While the ideal solution is to remove and replace Callery Pear with native fruit trees, that is not always an available option. The fruits can be harvested after the first frost, which makes them soft and edible—although seeds should still be avoided. Harvested fruit can be consumed directly from the tree or pureed and used to make pear butter and other preserves after removing seeds. Harvesting and consuming these pears might seem like a low return on time and energy, but it reduces the seed population available to birds that eat the fruit and contribute to spreading the invasive seeds.

QUICK REFERENCE:

USES: edible
FORAGE SEASON(S): late fall, winter
FORAGE PART(S): fruit
SPECIAL CONCERNS: Do not consume seeds.

OAK

Quercus spp.

PLANT: A large group of deciduous and evergreen shrubs and trees, notable for their fruit, a nut called an acorn.

LEAVES: Oak leaves are spirally arranged and display various leaf shapes. Many species have pointed or rounded lobes, while others are entire or serrate. Evergreen species are common in the milder parts of its range. The deciduous species often retain a significant portion of their leaves through the winter (marcescent).

FLOWERS: Oaks are monoecious, with flowers forming primarily in the leaf axils of new growth. Male flowers are catkins that are usually droopy or hanging. Female flowers are more inconspicuous and consist of a whorl of bracts (involucre) surrounding the ovary, with a protruding three-parted style.

FRUITS: A nut called an acorn. The size and shape of acorns vary by species, but typically they are round to ovate and are partially contained within a scaly cup, which is the remnant of the involucre. Acorns take one or two years to ripen, depending on the species.

ROOTS: The roots are shallow, typically not exceeding about 50 cm deep, but wide, often five to ten times the width of the canopy.

DISTRIBUTION AND HABITAT

At least 250 Oak species can be found throughout most of North America, from Panama north to central Alberta. The number of species may never be known because they readily hybridize and produce fertile offspring, making species identification problematic. They can be found in about every habitat, from deserts to rainforests.

FORAGING

Oak forage is very simple in some ways because, despite the variety of forms, acorns are very recognizable. Acorns can be gathered when you see them falling from the tree until the next spring—but the sooner the better, because you will be competing with the wildlife for your stash. One tricky part with acorns is the additional processing required to make them edible. Immediately after harvest, inspect your acorns for signs of tiny holes indicative of a worm infestation. Shell acorns and remove tannic acids through leaching.

If you do not want to use your acorns for flour, you can leach out the tannins using the boiled water method. Boil your acorns in 15-minute intervals, changing the water with each session until it remains clear and the acorn does not taste bitter. The slightly more labor-intensive method is cold water leaching, but it results in an end product that can be used in more applications because the acorn starches will not be cooked. Cold water leaching requires the dark skins to be removed from the acorns, and acorns should be macerated or ground. Next, transfer the ground acorns to a muslin bag—if this process is new to you, look for a product called a "nut milk bag"; they are reusable and inexpensive and just the trick for this job. Your acorn mush should be processed in cold running water to leach out the tannins. One relatively quick method is placing your nut milk bag in a strainer in your kitchen sink and just running the cold water over it until it is palatable. Another approach is to put your acorn mash into a sealable jar, cover it with water, seal the lid and refrigerate—changing the water multiple times daily. Some foragers place the mesh bag of acorn mush in their toilet tank to cold leach, but that is a rather polarizing option. When leaching is complete, squeeze out as much water as possible and dry at a temperature below 150° F. Once your product is dry, you can grind it into acorn flour and use it in various applications.

JAPANESE KNOTWEED
FLEECEFLOWER

Reynoutria japonica (formerly *Fallopia japonica*)

PLANT: A semi-woody perennial shrub, reaching up to 3 m in height. It forms dense thickets, spreading by rhizomes extending up to 20 m, and has hollow stems, like bamboo.

LEAVES: Leaves are alternate in arrangement and oval- to egg-shaped, with a pointed tip and broadly rounded base. They can get up to 15 cm long and 10 cm wide. The leaves are hairless and have entire margins. New leaves are often reddish, eventually fading to green. The leaf veins often retain some reddish coloration.

FLOWERS: Plants are dioecious, with flowers borne in erect clusters up to 15 cm long from the upper leaf axils. Individual flowers are small (up to 3 mm long), with five greenish to white petals. Male flowers have eight stamens; female flowers have three styles, each bearing vestigial organs of the opposite sex.

FRUITS: Fruits are three-angled, shiny brown or black achenes surrounded by three triangular, papery wings. Fruits are rarely produced because colonies tend to be unisexual due to extensive rhizomatous spreading.

ROOTS: The root system is fibrous with abundant, spreading rhizomes.

DISTRIBUTION AND HABITAT

Japanese Knotweed is native to East Asia but locally established in North America and Europe, where it is considered an invasive species. In North America, it is most abundant in the eastern half of the United States and southern Canada, as well as the Pacific Northwest and Northern Rockies. It is less common in the Great Plains and Southern Rockies. It grows most abundantly in well-drained, nutrient-rich soils and is commonly found in populated areas, gullies, roadsides, riverbanks, and pond edges.

FORAGING

Japanese Knotweed is an extremely invasive, fast-growing weed. The entire plant is edible, but the young stems are the most palatable and can be used in various ways. To make stems more palatable, they should be peeled to remove the fibrous outer layer. They can be processed like asparagus or pickled for longer-term preservation. Seeds and rhizomes are also edible.

QUICK REFERENCE:

USES: edible
FORAGE SEASON(S): spring, summer, fall
FORAGE PART(S): stems, seeds, rhizomes
SPECIAL CONCERNS: none

USES: edible

FORAGE SEASON(S): summer, fall, winter

FORAGE PART(S): fruit

SPECIAL CONCERNS: Do not confuse it with Poison Sumac (*Toxicodendron vernix*), which has white berries and does not look particularly similar to edible Sumac.

SUMAC

Rhus spp.

PLANT: A group of deciduous and evergreen shrubs and small trees in the Cashew family, reaching upwards of 10 m in height. They often form large clonal colonies through the spread of underground rhizomes.

LEAVES: Most species have pinnately compound leaves, often large in overall size, with a few species having either simple or trifoliate (compound with 3 leaflets) leaves. In most deciduous species, the leaves turn brilliant orange-red in the fall.

FLOWERS: Flowers are borne in dense spikes or panicles up to 30 cm long. Individual flowers are tiny and inconspicuous, with five petals that are typically greenish to white to pink in color.

FRUITS: Fruits are fleshy drupes that are variously covered with hair when ripe and are typically colored some shade of red, each containing one seed.

ROOTS: The root systems are primarily shallow and fibrous, but some species also produce root suckers, sometimes aggressively so.

DISTRIBUTION AND HABITAT

At least 27 species of Sumac may be found in North America, although many of those are non-native. As a whole, the genus is spread throughout most of North America, from Guatemala to central Canada. They can be found in a variety of habitats, although they are usually in moist, open habitats, such as woodland edges, prairies, old fields, and along roadsides and railways.

FORAGING

Sumac has large clusters of red berries that can be used to make a cold-processed tea or a spice. To make tea, remove berries from the large cluster and steep one cup of berries in a quart of cold water for 30 minutes. Try different methods and times to find a process that results in the flavor you most enjoy. Sumac spice can be harvested from fruits. To extract the spice, remove the berries from the cluster, grind whole berries in a food processor, and use a strainer to separate the fruit from the seed. You want to keep the fluffy red fruit surrounding the bland, hard berry. Sumac fruit can be further processed with other spices to create a unique seasoning. Sumac is commonly used in Middle Eastern cuisine.

SMOOTH SUMAC

Rhus glabra

KEY FEATURES

Widely distributed across the eastern half of the United States and adjacent parts of Canada, with much more scattered occurrences in the western half, primarily in the Pacific Northwest and Rocky Mountain regions. It is found in a variety of open to semi-open habitats, such as prairies, pastures, rock outcrops, roadsides, and forest openings. It is a spreading shrub that gets up to 3 m tall. The compound leaves have up to 31 leaflets. The flowers are yellowish to greenish, later becoming bright orange-red fruits that are no more than 6 mm in diameter and covered with short hairs.

STAGHORN SUMAC

Rhus typhina

KEY FEATURES

Widely distributed across the eastern half of the U.S. and adjacent parts of Canada, with more scattered populations to the west. It is found in habitats similar to *Rhus glabra* mentioned above. It is a shrub that is up to 5 m in height, with pinnately compound leaves with up to 31 leaflets. Twigs and petioles are covered by dense, short, reddish-brown hairs, resembling a deer's antlers when covered by velvet. Flowers are yellowish to greenish in color, while the fruits are tiny (~5 mm) and fuzzy, ripening to a deep red color.

CURRANTS
GOOSEBERRY

Ribes spp.

PLANT: Small to medium-sized erect or spreading shrubs, often with glandular-hairy stems. Some species also have spines and bristles on their stems.

LEAVES: Leaves of the various species are either palmately lobed or compound and may have hairy surfaces.

FLOWERS: Either solitary or in racemes or corymbs, and either terminal or axillary in location. The five sepals are often mistaken for the petals. They are longer than the petals and fused into a saucer- or cup-like shape. The much smaller petals are often the same color as the sepals, which can be white, yellow, pink, red, or purple, depending on the species.

FRUITS: The fruits are globose, many-seeded berries up to 2 cm in diameter. Color varies depending on the species, but most start greenish, ripening to some shade of red to purplish black. In some species, the fruits have prickles or glands on the otherwise smooth surface.

ROOTS: Most species have a shallow, fibrous root system.

DISTRIBUTION AND HABITAT

There are about 160 species of *Ribes*, 53 of which can be found in North America, and some cultivated varieties that can become adventive. You can expect to find *Ribes* species nearly anywhere in North America if you are in the right habitat. The various species occupy a broad range of habitat types. Still, they are generally found in areas with some shade, such as woodland edges and thickets, with some species performing better in wet soils than others.

FORAGING

Ribes are abundantly distributed throughout North America, and once you can identify one *Ribes*, you can identify other *Ribes*, at least to the genus level. One challenge in foraging and harvesting the *Ribes* is that the entire plant is covered in spines; in some species, even the fruit is covered in spines. It is advisable to gather wearing gloves and long sleeves to avoid injury. Spiny fruit should be processed before consumption, but fruit without spines can be eaten raw. Fruits can be used to make many different foods, including jellies, salsas, chutneys, and many more. With over 100 types of *Ribes*, as you gain experience foraging, you will adapt the use to fit the *Ribes* species.

GOLDEN CURRANT
PRUTERBERRY

Ribes aureum

KEY FEATURES

Native to the western part of North America, west of the Great Plains up to central Alberta. It has become adventive in eastern North America, as far east as Nova Scotia. It can be found in a variety of wooded and open habitats. It is a perennial shrub reaching up to 2.5 m in height. It is notable for having large, yellow flowers, lacking prickles, and having the largest leaves in the *Ribes* genus, up to 7 cm long and wide. The berry is around 1 cm in diameter and may be red, orange, yellow, brown, or black.

WAX CURRANT

Ribes cereum

KEY FEATURES

Native to the western half of the United States and Canada, where it is found in dry wood-lands and on rocky slopes. It has erect or arching stems up to 2 m in length. The stems are fuzzy and often covered with glandular hairs as well. Flowers are around 6 mm in width and cup-shaped, with the sepals curved back. The color ranges from greenish white to white to pinkish white. The ovoid berries are orange-red to red with a diameter of around 1 cm and usually lack flavor.

ROSE

Rosa spp.

PLANT: A large group of mostly deciduous, rhizomatous/stoloniferous (with modified stems below ground/above ground) shrubs and subshrubs, ranging in height from 0.1 m to 1 m. They may be erect, sprawling, or climbing in habit. Many species are armed with prickles or thorns.

LEAVES: Leaves are compound, with 3–13 elliptical to oblong leaflets.

FLOWERS: Flowers are borne in terminal panicles on the lateral shoots, containing anywhere from 1–50 flowers. The flowers are perfect in nearly every species, with five petals and up to 300 stamens. Flower color ranges from white to pink to red, although additional colors may be found in cultivated varieties.

FRUITS: *Rosa* species produce a type of aggregate fruit called a hip. They are spherical to oblong in shape, up to 2 cm in diameter, and can range in color from orange to red to purple to nearly black. Depending on the species, the hips may have glandular hairs on the outer surface or retain the sepals.

ROOTS: Two types of roots are found in *Rosa* species: thick, woody roots that support the main plant, and thin, fibrous roots that obtain water and minerals.

DISTRIBUTION AND HABITAT

Native and non-native species of Rose can be found throughout nearly the entirety of North America, in a wide variety of habitats.

FORAGING

All *Rosa* spp. produce edible fruits called hips. Rose hips can be processed for many edible uses. To process Rose hips, remove the stem and any remaining flower parts, bisect the fruit and scoop out the seeds. At this stage, the fruit can be dried or frozen for preservation. Fresh and frozen Rose hips can be used with other fruits in preserves, and dried Rose hips can be used for tea.

USES: edible

FORAGE SEASON(S): summer, fall

FORAGE PART(S): flowers, fruits

SPECIAL CONCERNS: Avoid thorns while harvesting Rose hips.

CAROLINA ROSE
PASTURE ROSE

Rosa carolina

KEY FEATURES

Carolina Rose is a native species across the eastern half of the United States and adjacent parts of southern Canada, out to Prince Edward Island. It is found in various habitats, including pastures, prairies, thickets, and open woodlands. This weak-stemmed species is mostly seen as a sprawling or semi-erect shrub, rarely more than 1 m tall. Stems have many paired prickles up to 1 cm long. The flowers are pink and up to 5.5 cm across. The hips are orange-red to red in color and globose in shape, around 1.5 cm in diameter. Most of the time, they will have a covering of stalked glands on the outer surface, and the sepals tend to fall off the hip soon after ripening.

SWEETBRIAR ROSE
EGLANTINE

Rosa
species of
interest

Rosa rubiginosa

KEY FEATURES

A native of Europe and western Asia, it has become established across most of North America, where it can be found along roadsides, in pastures, and other open areas. It is a dense, suckering shrub with long, arching stems up to 3 m tall that are densely covered with stout 1 cm–long prickles. The foliage is aromatic, with many describing it as apple-like. Flowers are up to 4 cm across and pink in color. Hips are dark red and oblong to pear-shaped, up to 25 mm in diameter.

MULTIFLORA ROSE

Rosa multiflora

KEY FEATURES

An east Asian native, it was widely planted throughout the U.S. in the early 1900s and has become established and invasive throughout most of North America. *Rosa multiflora* is found in the highest density across the eastern tier of the United States and adjacent areas of Canada, along the West Coast. It is located in disturbed areas, thickets, old pastures, streamsides, and forest edges. It may be erect or sprawling in habit, with stems up to 10 m long bearing many prickles. It has panicles of up to 30 white flowers (rarely pinkish) that are 2.5 cm wide. Hips are orangish to red, mostly spherical, with a diameter of 5–10 mm. They often have a sparse covering of stalked glands on the outer surface.

RASPBERRY
BLACKBERRY
THIMBLEBERRY
SALMONBERRY
AND MORE

Rubus spp.

PLANT: Biennial or perennial herbs and shrubs with arching to erect stems that are often armed with prickles or covered with hairs and glands.

LEAVES: Leaves may be simple or compound and generally spherical to elliptical. Leaf margins are usually serrated to some degree.

FLOWERS: Perfect flowers are borne in axillary or terminal clusters containing 1–100 flowers. They are five-parted and are either white or some shade of pink.

FRUITS: Fruits are aggregates of up to 150 drupelets that may or may not be coherent. They are colored white, yellow, pink, red, or black. Each drupelet contains one seed.

ROOTS: Root systems are typically woody, well-branched, and deeply penetrating. Some species form rhizomes.

DISTRIBUTION AND HABITAT

Rubus spp. are found throughout nearly all of North America, across many habitats.

FORAGING

Rubus spp. berries are an excellent forage food. Ripe berries will easily come off the plant. Berries can be eaten fresh or processed for jams, jellies, preserves, and baked goods. Leaves can be dried and used for tea.

> **QUICK REFERENCE:**
>
> **USES:** edible
> **FORAGE SEASON(S):** summer
> **FORAGE PART(S):** leaves, berries
> **SPECIAL CONCERNS:** none

BLACKBERRY

Rubus
species of
interest

Rubus allegheniensis

KEY FEATURES

Native to the eastern half of the U.S. and adjacent parts of Canada, in various wooded and non-wooded habitats. It is a biennial with stems that bear hairs, stalked glands, and stout prickles. The stems are erect to arching, up to 3 m long. Fruit is an aggregate of 20–100 black drupelets and is globose to cylindrical, up to 2 cm in diameter.

RASPBERRY

Rubus idaeus/strigosus

KEY FEATURES

Distributed throughout most of North America, primarily scarce or absent in the south-eastern United States. It is commonly found in fields, roadsides, and woodlands. It is generally accepted that there are two subspecies of *R. idaeus*: ssp. *idaeus* and ssp. *strigosus*. Ssp. *strigosus* is native to North America, while ssp. *idaeus* is native to Europe. Some botanists theorize the North American native is a separate species, *R. strigosus*. Regardless of who is correct, they are nearly identical, with the primary difference being the presence of stalked glands in the North American native. Otherwise, they are biennials, with erect stems up to 2.5 m long. The aggregate fruits are comprised of up to 60 drupelets and are red to whitish (occasionally amber), globular to conical in shape, and up to 2 cm in diameter.

THIMBLEBERRY

Rubus
species of
interest

Rubus parviflorus

KEY FEATURES

Thimbleberry is distributed across western North America, from approximately the U.S.-Mexico border to Juneau, Alaska. A disjunct population exists in the northern Great Lakes region, mostly around Lake Superior, Lake Huron, and northern Lake Michigan. It can be found in moist woods and thickets, streambanks, meadows, and dry, sandy sites like beaches and sand dunes. The stems can get up to 2 m tall and lack prickles. The leaves are palmately lobed, with 5–7 pointed lobes, and can be up to 30 cm long and wide. It has large, white flowers. The aggregate fruit is comprised of 50–60 drupelets ranging in color from pale pink to red. They are spherical, up to 1.8 cm in diameter.

SALMONBERRY

Rubus spectabilis

KEY FEATURES

Salmonberry is primarily a West Coastal species from the Gulf of Alaska to central California in moist woods, bogs, shorelines, and roadsides. It is a thicket-forming shrub, distinguished by its large, dark pink flowers. The aggregate fruit is comprised of 20–80 drupelets that are yellow, orange, or red. They are globular in shape, up to 2 cm in diameter.

DOCK
SORREL

Rumex spp.

PLANT: A large group of herbaceous annuals, biennials, and perennials, typically with inconspicuous flowers and weedy tendencies.

LEAVES: Leaves are alternate in arrangement, with some species also having a basal rosette of leaves. There is usually a membranous sheath around the stem where the leaf stalk attaches (ocrea). Leaf shape ranges from spherical to linear, with the leaves getting progressively smaller and narrower as you go up the stem. Leaf margins are mostly entire but may be undulate.

FLOWERS: Some species are monoecious, some are dioecious, and some have both unisexual and bisexual flowers on the same plant (polygamomonoecious). Flowers are borne in terminal and occasionally axillary panicles bearing numerous fascicles containing up to 30 flowers each. Flowers are bell-shaped with 5–6 dimorphic tepals that are green, pink, or red, six stamens, and three styles. Individual flowers are inconspicuous, typically no more than 6 mm long and wide.

FRUITS: Fruit is a single oblong achene encased within the tepals that dry and forms a papery, capsule-like structure. The capsule is usually tan to brown and may be winged.

ROOTS: Many species are tap-rooted, while others may be rhizomatous or stoloniferous.

DISTRIBUTION AND HABITAT

As a whole, *Rumex* can be found nearly everywhere in North America. There are around 200 species worldwide, with about 60 in North America, many of which are weedy non-natives. There is even one species native to the tundra of Alaska and northern Canada. Most species can be found in some kind of disturbed habitat, natural or manufactured, such as riverbanks, lakeshores, ditches, fields, and pastures.

FORAGING

Dock is one forage plant you either love or decide is not worth your time and energy for the bitter-tasting outcome. Young stems and leaves taste best. Very young leaves can be eaten raw, but older leaves should be boiled with at least one water change to make them palatable. Although Dock produces copious seeds that are easy to harvest and readily available to harvest late into the winter, it is very difficult to remove the husk. The most realistic strategy is to use the entire thing—husk and seed, grinding into a fine powder and using it as a partial flour substitute, no more than 25% of the flour called for should be replaced with Dock flour to avoid making your food too bitter to enjoy.

QUICK REFERENCE:

USES: edible, medicinal
FORAGE SEASON(S): spring, summer, fall, winter
FORAGE PART(S): stems, seeds
SPECIAL CONCERNS: none

QUICK REFERENCE:

USES: edible

FORAGE SEASON(S): spring (young leaves), late fall (corms and tubers)

FORAGE PART(S): young leaves, corms, tubers

SPECIAL CONCERNS: Some *Sagittaria* species are endangered, including *S. fasciculata* and *S. secundifolia*. Care should be used to ensure these endangered species are not harvested.

WAPATO
KATNISS
ARROWHEAD
DUCK POTATO
SWAN POTATO
TULE POTATO

Sagittaria latifolia

PLANT: Aquatic, emergent perennial reaching up to 100 cm tall.

LEAVES: Numerous basal, arrow-shaped leaves reaching up to 30 cm long.

FLOWERS: Long stalks over 100 cm tall bear racemes of male or female flowers. Male flowers have numerous bright yellow stamens and three white petals. Female flowers have multiple green stigmas clustered in a ball-like mass, surrounded by three white petals.

FRUITS: Achenes.

ROOTS: Shallow and fibrous. Long rhizomes, stolons, and corms may all be present.

DISTRIBUTION AND HABITAT

This species is distributed throughout the continental U.S. As an obligate wetland species, it grows in pond margins, wet open areas, swamps, and marshes. Although native to North America, it can become a weedy nuisance in some locations due to its ability to rapidly reproduce clonally and through copious seed production. It is a prohibited species in some parts of the world, including Australia and parts of Europe.

FORAGING

The common names of this species reference the historical use of this plant as a food source, with some archeological evidence of use dating back at least 4,500 years. Many First People across the North American continent harvested Wapato. One case study estimated that some Pacific Northwest locations harbored enough tubers in the late 19th century to provide 30,000 people with 20 percent of their annual calories. Harvest occurs in late fall after the plants have died back. A traditional harvest technique involves entering the water, sometimes neck deep, and digging with your feet and toes to dislodge corms and tubers from the muck. Once unearthed, corms and tubers rise to the surface and are loaded into a waiting canoe. Tubers and corms can safely be eaten raw, but the preferred method is to boil or roast for 30 minutes.

ELDERBERRY

Sambucus spp.

PLANT: *Sambucus* is a genus of shrubs and small trees ranging from 1–9 m in height.

LEAVES: Leaves are pinnately compound, comprised of 3–11 lance-elliptic leaflets with toothed margins. Leaves can reach up to 2 cm in length, depending on the species.

FLOWERS: Numerous small, white (rarely pink) flowers are borne on the tips of branches in flat or cone-shaped clusters. Flowers have 4–5 petals with an equal number of white-tipped stamens.

FRUITS: Small (5 mm) berries, ranging in color from black to blue or red, depending on the species.

ROOTS: Tend to form shallow, highly branched root systems.

DISTRIBUTION AND HABITAT

There are about 25 species of *Sambucus* found throughout most temperate and subtropical parts of the world, especially in the Northern Hemisphere. In North America, up to 12 species can be found, with nearly all parts being home to at least one species. Habitats differ between species, but they are primarily found in areas with some moisture, such as along the edges of marshes, ditches, floodplains, and mesic forests and meadows.

FORAGING

The flowers and berries of Elderberry are highly desirable forage finds. Depending on species and location, flowers can be seen as early as June and into July. Collect no more than 10 to 20 percent of the flowers per tree. Flowers can be used fresh to infuse syrup or various other recipes. Flowers can also be dried and stored for teas and flavoring. In late summer and early fall, berries can be harvested. After harvest, berries should be removed from stems and processed into jams, syrups, or frozen for later use. Blue and Black Elderberry are sweeter and more desirable than Red Elderberry, which has a bitter taste but is not poisonous. It is generally not advised to eat raw berries from any *Sambucus* species.

QUICK REFERENCE:

USES: edible, medicinal

FORAGE SEASON(S): spring, summer, fall

FORAGE PART(S): flowers, fruit

SPECIAL CONCERNS: Bark, seeds, and leaves are cyanogenic. Some foragers report that stomach upset occurs after consuming raw berries. *Sambucus racemosa* is often reported to be more poisonous than other *Sambucus* species and may cause gastrointestinal distress if consumed in large quantities. It is safest to consume berries of all *Sambucus* species after cooking.

QUICK REFERENCE:

USES: edible

FORAGE SEASON(S): spring, summer, fall

FORAGE PART(S): leaves

SPECIAL CONCERNS: Root and bark material contain safrole, a known carcinogen.

SASSAFRAS

Sassafras albidum

PLANT: An aromatic deciduous tree reaching up to 35 m in height. The bark of mature trees is reddish-brown and furrowed. They often form dense thickets due to the tendency to produce sprouts from underground runners. The northern parts of its range tend to be more shrub-like than treelike.

LEAVES: Leaves are alternately arranged, and ovate to elliptical with an entire margin. They grow up to 16 cm long and 10 cm wide. The leaves may be unlobed or have 2–3 lobes. All three leaf shapes can be found on the same branch.

FLOWERS: Sassafras is dioecious, with flowers borne in drooping axillary racemes containing just a few flowers before leafing out. They have 5–6 greenish-yellow tepals. Male flowers have nine stamens, and female flowers have six sterile stamens and a slender style with a capitate stigma.

FRUITS: The fruit is a dark blue, roundish drupe, about 1 cm in diameter, on a pinkish-red, fleshy, club-shaped pedicel. The fruit ripens in late summer and contains one seed.

ROOTS: The root system is shallow (<50 cm) and laterally spreading, up to 75 cm per year. They readily form new shoots and can form dense thickets through suckering.

DISTRIBUTION AND HABITAT

Sassafras is found in the eastern half of the United States and southern Ontario. It ranges from southwestern Maine to central Michigan, southward to eastern Oklahoma and Texas, and west to northern Florida. They are usually found in old fields and woodland openings, with a preference for moist but well-drained soils.

FORAGING

Sassafras, as an edible, is probably best known for its use in Creole cooking. Sassafras leaves are used to make filé powder, a seasoning and thickening agent used in traditional filé gumbo. It is very easy to prepare filé powder. Harvest leaves and allow them to dry in a cool, dark location. Once leaves are dry, process with a mortar and pestle or food processor to grind to a fine powder. Store powder in a dry place for up to a year.

GREENBRIER
CATBRIER
CARRION FLOWER

Smilax spp.

PLANT: A group of shrubs, vines, and herbs that tend to be sprawling or climbing in growth habit. They may be deciduous or evergreen, and some species are armed with prickles. They often form dense, impenetrable thickets.

LEAVES: Leaf shape ranges from linear to oblong to heart-shaped, often with a lobed base and alternate. They may be covered with many short hairs, especially on the lower leaf surface. Tendrils are present in most species, although they are rudimentary in a few species.

FLOWERS: Inflorescences are usually round or umbellate clusters that hang from the stem and alternate to the leaves. Depending on the species, the clusters may be few-flowered or have up to 100 (or more) flowers. Plants are dioecious, often growing in colonies of the same sex. Individual flowers are six-parted, with six greenish or yellowish tepals. Male flowers have six stamens, and female flowers have six staminodes and a three-parted stigma.

FRUITS: Fruits are 5–10 mm wide berries and may be colored black, blue, purple, red, or orange.

ROOTS: *Smilax* typically have very extensive root systems, developing large tubers and spreading rhizomes.

DISTRIBUTION AND HABITAT

Smilax spp. are found worldwide, primarily in tropical and subtropical areas. There are about 20 species native to North America, mainly in the eastern half of Canada and the U.S. and throughout Mexico, with another population cluster centered around Northern California and Southern Oregon. The various species occur in a wide range of upland and wetland habitats.

FORAGING

All *Smilax* species are edible, and all parts of the plant are safe to consume. Berries can be eaten raw, but the large seed makes raw consumption inconvenient, and many *Smilax* species are covered in sharp thorns, making berry harvest significantly more challenging. When used, berries are processed into juice and jelly. Young stems and leaves can be used as fresh greens in salads. The large tuber roots can be dried and ground into powder; different *Smilax* species have unique root properties resulting in various flavor properties and uses based on species. Despite reports of historical use by certain Indigenous people of North America, many modern foragers report that obtaining starch from *Smilax* roots is not energy efficient.

QUICK REFERENCE:

USES: edible, medicinal
FORAGE SEASON(S): spring, summer
FORAGE PART(S): berries, roots
SPECIAL CONCERNS: none

SAW GREENBRIER

Smilax bona-nox

KEY FEATURES

Distributed across the southeast quadrant of the United States into eastern Mexico, in forests, fields, thickets, and hedgerows. It is a prickly perennial, evergreen vine capable of reaching the tops of neighboring trees. The leaves are lanceolate to triangular, often with white blotches.

CATBRIER

Smilax rotundifolia

KEY FEATURES

Distributed from New England to the southern Great Lakes region and south-central Texas, in woodlands and thickets. It is a woody perennial vine that may be deciduous or evergreen, reaching lengths of up to 6 m. The stems are covered in prickles up to 12 mm long. Leaves are usually broadly ovate, up to 17 cm long and wide.

SMOOTH CARRION FLOWER

Smilax herbacea

KEY FEATURES

Found primarily from New England to the southern Great Lakes region and southern Appalachia, in rich woods and thickets. It is an annual vine that lacks prickles, up to 2.5 m long, with ovate to round leaves.

BASSWOOD
LINDEN

Tilia spp.

PLANT: A group of deciduous trees in the Mallow family that can get up to 40 m in height with a 20 m wide crown on a strong, straight trunk up to 1 m in diameter. They are notable wildlife-attracting trees, with various types of organisms readily using leaves, flowers, fruits, and sap as food sources.

LEAVES: Leaves are alternate in arrangement and ovate to heart-shaped with a finely serrated margin and are usually slightly asymmetrical. They are 5–20 cm long and 5–12 cm wide.

FLOWERS: Flowers are borne in erect or drooping clusters attached to a linear bract that grows from the leaf axils of first-year twigs after leaf emergence. The flowers are radially symmetrical, with five sepals and five petals, typically yellowish-white in color. There may be anywhere from 30–60 stamens in the center of the flower surrounding a single white style with a five-lobed stigma.

FRUITS: The fruit is a round, hard, nut-like berry. Minute hairs cover the outer surface, turning grayish tan when ripe.

ROOTS: Basswoods tend to have deep and widely-spreading root systems.

DISTRIBUTION AND HABITAT

There is one native species in North America, *Tilia americana*, and at least four non-native species, one of which is a common landscape tree (*Tilia cordata*). They are predominantly found east of the Rocky Mountains in the U.S., Canada, and south-central Mexico. It is observed in woodland habitats across its range, seemingly preferring rich, mesic soils.

FORAGING

Tilia spp. are an interesting forage tree that are often overlooked. All parts of the tree are edible. Young leaves and leaf buds can be eaten raw as fresh greens. Flowers can be dried and used in teas and tinctures. *Tilia* spp. seeds are edible, but some are more desirable than others. Some species are reported to have seeds with chocolate or coffee-like properties. Sap and bark can also be harvested, but the practicality and sustainability are debatable. *Tilia* spp. sap contains less than half the sugar of a Maple species, making it much less efficient and practical to process into syrup. I rarely recommend foraging bark for any tree species because it generally increases the risk of disease in the tree and is not a sustainable practice in most cases.

QUICK REFERENCE:

USES: edible
FORAGE SEASON(S): spring, summer
FORAGE PART(S): leaves, flowers, seeds
SPECIAL CONCERNS: none

QUICK REFERENCE:

USES: edible
FORAGE SEASON(S): spring, possibly late fall, winter
FORAGE PART(S): leaves, roots
SPECIAL CONCERNS: none

SALSIFY
OYSTER PLANT
PURPLE GOATSBEARD

Tragopogon porrifolius

PLANT: An herbaceous biennial or perennial up to 1.5 m in height in the Aster family.

LEAVES: It has both basal and stem leaves that are long and narrow with parallel veins, resembling blades of grass. They range in length from 5 to 20 cm. The stem leaves are alternately arranged with clasping bases. The leaves are fleshy and exude a milky sap when crushed.

FLOWERS: A solitary flower forms at the tip of the stem. It is of the composite type and can get up to 5 cm across. The disc and ray flowers are dull or pale purple. The flower is subtended (beneath the flower) by 8–9 narrow, pointed bracts that are longer than the ray flower petals.

FRUITS: Mature fruiting bodies resemble dandelions, with a cluster of small cylindrical achenes (~20 mm long) with a tuft of hair on the outward pointing tip that facilitates wind dispersal.

ROOTS: It has a thick, fleshy taproot up to 30 cm long and 5 cm wide.

DISTRIBUTION AND HABITAT

In North America, *T. porrifolius* is abundant along the West Coast. There are more scattered populations in the Rocky Mountains and eastern Great Lakes. It is mostly found in disturbed grounds, such as roadsides and agricultural areas, usually in soils that are somewhat moist.

FORAGING

All *Tragopogon* spp. found in North America have edible leaves and roots, but the exotic species *T. porrifolius* is thought to be the tastiest and to have the largest harvestable roots. The trick with foraging for this genus is that it is most palatable before flowering, which makes identification a little more challenging. Young leaves can be eaten raw or blanched, and roots can be harvested before flowering occurs. Some sources also recommend harvesting after a hard frost to improve flavor.

WATER CALTROP
BAT NUT
DEVIL'S NUT
MUSTACHE NUT
WATER CHESTNUT

Trapa natans

PLANT: An annual, floating aquatic plant with a submerged stem up to 5 m long that anchors to the riverbed/lakebed. It can form dense mats on the surface of the water, with up to three layers of plants.

LEAVES: Floating leaves form a rosette of small ovoid or rhombic-shaped leaves with serrated margins, approximately 0.5 cm long and wide (usually wider than long). They are attached to inflated petioles that may be up to 20 cm long. The lower surface of these leaves are covered in silky hairs. Submerged leaves are found alternately arranged along the upper part of the stem. They are small and linear in shape.

Below the submerged leaves on the stem are whorls of adventitious, feathery roots reminiscent of water milfoil leaves.

FLOWERS: Solitary flowers are borne from the central axils of the floating rosette. They have four white petals and are no more than 30 mm wide.

FRUITS: The fruit is a hard drupe, up to 4 cm in diameter, containing one seed. It has four barbed, sharp spines approximately 1 cm long. These spines are strong enough to penetrate most footwear.

ROOTS: Roots are long and thin and grow straight down into the muck to anchor the plant in the water.

DISTRIBUTION AND HABITAT

A native of Europe, Asia, and Africa, it has become established and invasive in the northeast part of the U.S. and adjacent areas of Canada, from the Outer Banks of North Carolina to Ottawa and Montreal. It is found in nutrient-rich rivers and lakes, up to 5 m deep water.

FORAGING

Trapa natans is an introduced invasive aquatic plant species that produce large, floating mats of plant material that disrupt the freshwater ecology of the locations they invade. This plant is a highly desired forage species in some parts of Europe. One Polish forager called it a "floating buffet," and it has been harvested to the point of endangerment in Germany. In North America, it has been reported in freshwater lakes and great lakes tributaries in the northeastern United States, and its removal is a top priority. Fruits are

harvestable in summer and fall and can be found floating attached to large rosettes of leaves. Fruits are large and unmistakable. Although the fruit is edible raw, it is safer to boil these before consuming them to reduce toxins and exposure to a parasitic fluke.

QUICK REFERENCE:

USES: edible

FORAGE SEASON(S): summer, fall

FORAGE PART(S): fruit

SPECIAL CONCERNS: This is a destructive, invasive weed and should not be transported outside of the infested area.

QUICK REFERENCE:

USES: edible, medicinal
FORAGE SEASON(S): fall
FORAGE PART(S): berries
SPECIAL CONCERNS: none

WILD COFFEE
HORSE GENTIAN
FEVERWORT
TINKER'S WEED

Triosteum **spp.**

PLANT: Herbaceous perennial plants in the Honeysuckle family. They have hairy stems and reach up to 1.2 m in height.

LEAVES: Leaves are opposite in arrangement and connate (lower lobes of each leaf pair are fused) or perfoliate, with the bases of each pair of leaves joining and attaching to and encircling the stem. Leaf pairs stick out at a 90° angle to the leaf pair below it. The broadly elliptical leaves can get up to 25 cm long and 10 cm wide and are often softly hairy.

FLOWERS: Flowers are borne from the leaf axils or in racemes at the stem tip. Flowers are stalkless and tubular, often having a velvety appearance, and tend to point outwards from the leaf axils. They have five round lobes at the open end, which mostly conceal the stamens, with just a single style emerging beyond the lobes. Flower color ranges from yellowish to brownish-red. The five sepals are typically hairy and very narrow, with a pointed tip, often longer than the flower itself.

FRUITS: Fruits are round drupes, with the five sepals persisting on the outer surface. Ripe fruit color varies among the species but is either white, yellow, orange, or red. Within each drupe is one large, hard seed.

ROOTS: The root system consists of a thick, fleshy taproot with many horizontal branches.

DISTRIBUTION AND HABITAT

In North America, the three native *Triosteum* species are found almost entirely in the eastern half of the U.S., minus the southeastern states, and southern Manitoba and Quebec. Preferred habitats are mostly rich woodlands, shady riverbanks, and prairies, and they tend to be absent from especially degraded areas.

FORAGING

Many foragers agree that Wild Coffee is not a quality substitute for coffee, but it is interesting to find the plant and try it for oneself. Fruits of *T. perfoliatum* can be harvested in late summer or early fall. Cut into smaller pieces and bake at 150° F until dry to prepare fruits to be used as a coffee substitute. Grind dried plant material in a coffee bean grinder and steep in boiling water for 3–5 minutes. The roots of *Triosteum* species are used medicinally as a general tonic, to reduce fever, and to treat colds and flu.

CAT TAIL
CATTAIL

Typha spp.

PLANT: Perennial, herbaceous plants of primarily wetland habitats that can reach over 3 m in height, often forming dense stands.

LEAVES: Thick, linear, and ribbon-like, with numerous air channels within, giving them a spongy feel.

FLOWERS: Monoecious, in dense racemes at the ends of vertical stems. Male flowers are densely packed into a narrow spike near the end of the stem, senescing (falling) after the pollen is shed. Female flowers are densely packed into a more prominent brown, sausage-like spike immediately beneath the male flowers, often persisting into winter. When ripe, the female spike readily falls apart into a cottony mass of seeds.

FRUITS: Seeds are tiny, up to 2 mm long, with several wispy white hairs attached to facilitate wind dispersal.

ROOTS: Tuberous, white, and rhizomatous.

DISTRIBUTION AND HABITAT

Worldwide, there are 30 species of *Typha*. In North America, three species are present. All three species readily hybridize in areas where they are growing together. They are primarily found in fresh and slightly brackish wetlands, usually in muck or shallow water (up to 1.5 m deep), along the margins of bays, lakes, and slow-moving rivers.

FORAGING

Cattail is a versatile plant that can be an excellent source of protein and carbohydrates. The leaves and mature female flowers can be used as building materials and insulation. It is a good "starter" forage plant for the beginner as it is abundant and invasive in some areas. It is easy to identify, and different parts can be harvested almost any time of year. In early spring, young stem shoots can be gathered by pulling out the plant and removing the surrounding outer leaves, revealing tender, white shoots at the base of the plant. Although shoots are not toxic raw, it is safest to consume shoots after they have been pickled or sauteed to avoid waterborne pathogens such as *Escherichia coli* and *Giardia*. Some foragers will also harvest the tender sprouts growing off roots in early spring. Immature male and female flowers can be harvested, prepared, and consumed like corn on the cob. From May to June, pollen can be harvested from the male catkins. The window of opportunity for pollen harvest is brief; after pollen is released, the male flowers wither away. To harvest the pollen, gather male catkins when the bright yellow pollen first appears on the outer surface and shake the flowers into a storage container to collect

pollen—be prepared for a copious release of pollen. After collection, pollen should be sifted to remove debris, and then it can be stored in a cool, dry place for up to six months. Cattail pollen can replace up to half the wheat flour in many recipes.

In late summer, fall and winter, Cattail rhizomes can be harvested by digging into the muck and pulling them out of the ground. Begin digging at the base of the stem to get to the rhizome. Harvesting rhizomes is a messy and sometimes cold job, so come prepared! Rhizomes are fibrous and tough and cannot be eaten raw. There are a few methods for separating starch from rhizome fibers. A simple and easy field method is to clean, peel, and roast the rhizome, chewing around the fibers to obtain starch. A longer-term storage method involves cleaning and peeling the rhizome, shredding the fibers lengthwise, placing fibers in a container of water, and wringing them out in the water to extract the starch. After several hours the starch will settle to the bottom, the water can then be poured off, and the remaining starch can be dried, stored, and used to replace up to half the flour in many standard recipes.

Many cultures have used leaves to create baskets, hats, and other valuable items. Seeds from mature flower heads are used as insulating material.

QUICK REFERENCE:

USES: edible, fiber, baskets

FORAGE SEASON(S): spring, summer, fall, winter

FORAGE PART(S): rhizomes, catkins, stems, pollen

SPECIAL CONCERNS: *Iris* species are toxic look-alikes, especially in early spring.

STINGING NETTLE

Urtica gracilis (formerly *U. dioica*)

PLANT: Herbaceous perennial plants, up to 3 m in height. They may be single-stemmed or multi-branched and either erect or sprawling in habit. Leaves and stems are covered with hollow hairs that act like hypodermic needles, injecting a chemical concoction into the skin when touched, resulting in a burning or stinging sensation.

LEAVES: The oppositely arranged leaves are lanceolate or elliptical (sometimes narrowly so), up to 20 cm long and 13 cm wide, but mostly about half that size. The leaf margins are coarsely serrated.

FLOWERS: Plants can be either monoecious or dioecious, with the flowers borne in dense clusters on long, drooping panicles. Individual flowers are four-parted, small, and non-showy, with greenish-yellow floral parts. Male flowers tend to be on more erect peduncles, while female flowers are more lax.

FRUITS: The fruits are ovoid achenes, approximately 1.5 mm x 1 mm.

ROOTS: Plants have a wide-spreading network of bright yellow stolons and rhizomes, with many fibrous roots. They can spread laterally up to 2 m in one growing season, often resulting in large, dense patches.

DISTRIBUTION AND HABITAT

Stinging Nettles are found throughout nearly all of North America, seemingly absent only in Hawaii and areas south of Mexico City. They can be found in various habitats, typically in rich, moist soil. Common habitats include streams, riverbanks, lakeshores, rich and moist forests, wet meadows, and wetland edges.

FORAGING

Stinging Nettle is sometimes called "the plant of 1,000 uses." The stems and leaves can be boiled in the spring for nutritious fresh greens. Leaves can be collected and dried for tea and infusions with numerous pharmacological applications, including improved cardiovascular health and anti-inflammatory and anti-hypertensive effects. While the extent of the medicinal benefits of *Urtica* spp. is still being determined, it is deemed a safe prophylactic treatment.

Stinging Nettle is also used to produce strong fibers for the production of rope and fabric. You can forage *Urtica* stems and process them yourself. First, collect stems and soak them for at least a week to rot off the non-fibrous materials. After soaking, allow stems to dry completely and then break off any remaining non-fibrous materials to extract the fibers. After you have extracted your fibers, run the fibers over hackles (boards with long nails) to separate the short fibers from the long fibers. From this point, the fibers need to be spun into yarn and woven into cloth.

QUICK REFERENCE:

USES: edible, medicinal, fiber

FORAGE SEASON(S): spring, summer, fall

FORAGE PART(S): stem, leaves

SPECIAL CONCERNS: Plant hairs contain irritating compounds that burn and sting skin on contact.

BLUEBERRY
CRANBERRY
BILBERRY
WHORTLEBERRY
HUCKLEBERRY
LINGONBERRY

Vaccinium

PLANT: A large group of subshrubs, shrubs, vines, and trees. Stems can be erect, spreading, creeping, and often woody or hairy.

LEAVES: Leaves may be persistent or deciduous, with generally an elliptical shape. Leaf margins can be entire or serrated and are revolute (in-rolled) in some species. Leaf surfaces range from hairless to hairy and have brochidodromous venation, where the secondary leaf veins are connected via loops or arches rather than terminating at the leaf margin.

FLOWERS: Flowers are either four- or five-petaled, with the petals fusing and forming a bell- or urn-shaped tube. Flower color ranges from white to pink, red, or green. They are found in terminal or axillary racemes of 2–10 flowers.

FRUITS: Fruit is an oval or round, fleshy berry containing 2–40 elliptical seeds. They are usually brightly colored blue or red, with most species having a sweet taste.

ROOTS: Most species form dense, highly branched networks of delicate roots.

DISTRIBUTION AND HABITAT

There are 500 species of *Vaccinium*, 25 of which are found in North America. Most species are found primarily on mountain slopes in tropical regions. The remaining species are found in temperate and boreal regions of the Northern Hemisphere, occupying a variety of habitats, mostly on acidic soils in such habitats as bogs, sandhills, coniferous woods, alpine meadows, glades, and talus slopes.

FORAGING

Blueberries are an excellent forage food for beginners. They are straightforward to identify with no poisonous look-alikes. The hardest part about Blueberry forage is finding a good patch, with large, wild populations most likely distributed in specific habitats in rural, undisturbed locations. Michigan, Maine, and Canada still have commercial harvests from wild populations of Blueberry. Blueberries make excellent dried fruit, jams, jellies, and pies.

QUICK REFERENCE:

USES: edible
FORAGE SEASON(S): summer
FORAGE PART(S): berries
SPECIAL CONCERNS: none

LOWBUSH BLUEBERRY

Vaccinium
species of
interest

Vaccinium angustifolium

KEY FEATURES

Lowbush Blueberry is native from the Great Lakes to New England, adjacent areas of Canada, and southward down the Appalachians. They can be found in dry, sandy habitats such as barrens, outcrops, and dry forests, as well as in bogs. These small deciduous shrubs reach up to 40 cm tall and often form dense colonies. They have white, urn-shaped flowers followed by small blue berries up to 1 cm in diameter.

HIGHBUSH BLUEBERRY

Vaccinium corymbosum

KEY FEATURES

Highbush Blueberry is distributed from New England to the Southern Appalachians and southern Great Lakes. Common habitats include bogs, lake and stream banks, pine barrens, and mountain summits. It is a deciduous shrub, up to 4 m tall. Flowers are barrel-shaped and white or pink, followed by blue to black berries up to 1.5 cm in diameter.

CRANBERRY

Vaccinium macrocarpon

KEY FEATURES

Cranberry is distributed from the Great Lakes to New England and southward in the Appalachians and parts of the Pacific Northwest. It is primarily found in sphagnum or sedge bogs and sandy lakeshores. Plants are sprawling or ascending, up to 15 cm high, with small, thick leaves up to 0.5 cm long. Flowers are white or pink, with reflexed (pointed backwards) petals, followed by a pinkish-red berry up to 1.5 cm in diameter.

LINGONBERRY
PARTRIDGEBERRY

Vaccinium
species of
interest

Vaccinium vitis-idaea

KEY FEATURES

Lingonberry is distributed from Alaska to New England. It is found in habitats such as muskegs, bogs, tundra, cliffs, and mountain summits. Flowers are cup-shaped and pinkish-white in color, followed by shiny red berries up to 1 cm in diameter.

CORN SALAD
LAMB'S LETTUCE
MACHE

Valerianella locusta

PLANT: A small, herbaceous annual plant, growing up to 0.3 m in height and width. They grow as a basal rosette of leaves, from which multiple branching flower stems emerge. The stems are four-angled and pubescent (short, soft hairs) with retrorse (downward-pointing) hairs.

LEAVES: Basal leaves form a rosette, are spatulate (spoon-shaped), and can reach up to 15 cm in length and 2 cm in width. They are typically hairless, but some individuals are sparsely pubescent. Stem leaves are opposite in arrangement, sessile, and lanceolate to oblong shape, reducing in size as you move up the stem. They tend to have a fringe of short hairs along their margin.

FLOWERS: Flowers are borne in terminal cymose clusters during spring. They are funnel-shaped, up to 1 mm long and 1.5 mm across, with five spreading petals and 2–3 stamens. Each flower is subtended (growing beneath) by two oblong bracts up to 3 mm long. With lots of sunshine, the tips of the bracts often become reddish. The flower color is usually pale blue but can be pink or nearly pure white.

FRUITS: Fruit is a 2–3 mm long achene. Each achene has three chambers, two of which are sterile (empty). The fertile chamber is noticeably thickened by a corky mass.

ROOTS: This species has a thin taproot, from which smaller, fibrous roots emanate.

DISTRIBUTION AND HABITAT

Native to Europe, it has been widely cultivated worldwide. It can be found in North America, primarily in the Pacific Northwest and in a broad swath from Nova Scotia to Texas. It can be found in various habitats, including woodlands, meadows, fields, roadsides, and waste places.

FORAGING

Corn Salad is an escaped cultivated plant commonly grown in European kitchen gardens and is now also found in western and eastern North America. Although this plant is a bit trickier to identify as it is best to harvest before flowering occurs, it is very tender and tasty and worth adding to your repertoire. It is also a rare forage green available in the cooler seasons, depending on your growing zone. It is primarily a cooler season green that tends to be more commonly observed in towns and cities than in rural areas. Leaves are harvested before flowering, washed, and eaten raw.

MULLEIN
VELVET PLANT
FLANNEL PLANT

Verbascum thapsus

PLANT: An herbaceous biennial that can reach up to 2 m in height, occasionally taller. Nearly all parts of the plant are covered with short, stellate hairs, which give it a fuzzy gray or silver appearance.

LEAVES: First-year leaves form a basal rosette with a maximum leaf size of up to 50 cm long and 15 cm wide. The leaves are generally oval-shaped, with a blunt tip, and feel like velvet or flannel due to the dense covering of hairs and the thick leaf blade. Second-year plants grow a tall, narrow flowering stem with alternate leaves. The stem leaves are similar to the basal leaves and get progressively smaller as you go up the stem. The base of each leaf tapers to a winged stalk that extends downward on the stem (decurrent leaf).

FLOWERS: Flowers are borne in a densely packed spike up to 60 cm long at the end of the stem. Individual flowers are approximately 2 cm across, with five densely hairy sepals, five yellow petals, five orange-tipped stamens, and one curved green style. Only a few flowers are open at any given time, beginning from the bottom of the spike. Occasionally, shorter secondary flower spikes may grow out from the base of the primary spike.

FRUITS: Fruit is a roundish capsule that splits in two upon ripening. Each capsule contains up to 800 tiny, six-sided pitted seeds. One flowering spike can produce up to 300 capsules. Seeds can remain viable for many decades, if not longer. Dead flower stalks often persist through winter.

ROOTS: The plant produces a deep taproot with fibrous secondary roots.

DISTRIBUTION AND HABITAT

Native to Europe, North Africa, and Asia, it has been introduced to many other parts of the world. In North America, it can be found, often abundantly, from southern Canada to northern Mexico. It is most often found in dry soils in full sun, usually in disturbed areas with minimal competition from other plants, because the seeds require light to germinate.

FORAGING

Leaves and flowers can be harvested in the spring. Most frequently, they are dried and ground for tea and medicinal applications. Roots are harvested in the fall and, like leaves and flowers, are processed by cutting into small parts, drying, and grinding into a powder for teas. Sometimes the dried plant materials are smoked for medicinal reasons, including treatment for asthma or coughs—some herbalists recommend this seemingly counterintuitive strategy because it allows the medicine to enter directly into the lungs.

QUICK REFERENCE:

USES: edible, medicinal
FORAGE SEASON(S): spring, summer, fall
FORAGE PART(S): leaves, flowers, root
SPECIAL CONCERNS: none

VIOLET

Viola spp.

PLANT: A large group of mostly low-growing herbaceous annuals and perennials. Many species lack visible stems, with their leaves and flower stalks emerging from underground stolons or rhizomes.

LEAVES: In species that have stems, the leaves are alternate in arrangement, typically a basal rosette of leaves in addition to the stem leaves. Leaf shape is variable, but most species have simple leaves ranging from linear, orbiculate, ovate, lanceolate, heart-shaped, or kidney-shaped. Some species have deeply lobed or dissected leaves.

FLOWERS: Flowers are primarily produced early in the growing season and are bilaterally symmetrical. They are mainly solitary, emerging from the leaf axils of the stems or the rhizome or stolon. They are mostly showy and have five petals: two upper petals, two lateral petals, and one lower petal with a nectar spur. The inner surface of at least the lateral petals are bearded, with various types of short hairs. The stamens converge over the ovary, forming a cone-shaped structure. The flower color is variable amongst the species, with white, yellow, blue, and pink being the most common. Many species are bi- or tri-colored and have prominent darker veins on lateral and lower petals.

FRUITS: Round to elliptical capsules containing 6–75 roundish seeds. Upon maturing, the capsules split open, dispersing the seeds ballistically. Many species have a fleshy cap or covering on the seeds that ants readily bring to their nests to feed their young, thereby further dispersing the seeds.

ROOTS: Annual species tend to be shallowly tap-rooted, while perennial species are usually rhizomatous or stoloniferous.

DISTRIBUTION AND HABITAT

There are around 700 *Viola* species distributed nearly worldwide, with about 100 species present in North America, many of which are non-native. As a whole, *Viola* is distributed throughout almost the entirety of North America. Most species are primarily found in moist, shady areas of rich woods and wetlands. However, many species are adapted to much drier and open habitats, such as prairies and barrens.

FORAGING

All *Viola* spp. flowers are edible and can be used to make elegant jellies and candies. Refer to Fireweed (page 64) for additional information.

QUICK REFERENCE:

USES: edible
FORAGE SEASON(S): spring, summer
FORAGE PART(S): flowers
SPECIAL CONCERNS: none

GRAPE

Vitis spp.

PLANT: Mostly woody vines (lianas), although some species appear more shrub-like. They have exfoliating bark and a brown pith (plant tissue in central part of the stem). Mature vines can become rather large, up to 50 cm in diameter, and often grow high into the canopy of neighboring trees.

LEAVES: Leaves can vary between the species and even on individual plants. Leaves are long-stalked and relatively large, up to 25 cm long and wide. They may be deeply or shallowly lobed and often have serrated and hairy margins. On first-year growth, tendrils develop opposite the leaves, usually every third leaf.

FLOWERS: Flowers are borne opposite the leaves in clusters technically termed thyrses. A thyrse is where the main stem of the cluster is racemose, but the secondary stems/stalks are cymose. Lilacs and Horse Chestnuts are other examples of thyrses. Individual flowers are either male or female, with clusters being all-male, all-female, or mixed. Individual flowers are five-parted and tend to be small, with fused petals that fall off soon after opening. Male flowers will have five long, erect stamens around a button-like center. Female flowers have a short, stubby style surrounded by five usually sterile stamens that are contorted or otherwise disfigured. Flowers in most species are noticeably fragrant.

FRUITS: Purple or black berries containing 1–4 seeds. Some cultivated varieties have white or green berries.

ROOTS: The root system is densely branched and woody, with most of the roots within 1 m of the surface, although individual roots can penetrate down to a depth of 9 m.

DISTRIBUTION AND HABITAT

Vitis spp. can be found throughout most North America, from southern Canada to the Caribbean Islands and Panama. Habitats vary from species to species, but most tend to be found in thickets, forest edges, and riparian areas.

FORAGING

Grapes are abundant and easy to identify. Leaves can be harvested throughout the spring and summer. Due to the fibrous, tough qualities of the Grape leaves, they are usually prepared by fermenting and used to make stuffed Grape leaves and dolmas. Tendrils can be harvested throughout the growing season and added to fresh greens or eaten directly from the vine; I once had a traditional healer tell me that he prescribes Grape vine tendrils to his patients who need a little extra energy. They have a tangy, refreshing burst of flavor. The fruits can be harvested by cutting large bunches directly off the vine. Some choose to wait until after a freeze to reduce bitterness, but this is a matter of personal preference. After harvesting, Grape bunches should be washed and processed. Typically, processing involves mashing Grapes in a large cooking vessel, adding enough water to cover the grapes, and heating to release juices. Straining at least twice helps to remove tartaric acid crystals and generally improves the flavor. Grape juice can be further processed in a variety of applications, including jelly and wine.

QUICK REFERENCE:

USES: edible

FORAGE SEASON(S): spring, summer, fall

FORAGE PART(S): leaves, tendrils, fruit

SPECIAL CONCERNS: It can be confused with the poisonous plant Canada Moonseed, *Menispermum canadense*. Canada Moonseed fruits contain a single, crescent-shaped seed in each fruit. Edible grapes contain two to four smaller, pear-shaped seeds.

COONTIE PALM
FLORIDA ARROWROOT

Zamia integrifolia

PLANT: A woody, shrub-like evergreen cycad, with most (if not all) of the stem underground. Above-ground height is from 30–90 cm, with a width of 90–150 cm.

LEAVES: The leaves grow from the tip of the underground stem. They are pinnately compound, up to 130 cm long. Each leaf is comprised of 5–30 stiff, dark, glossy green leaflets, each up to 17 cm long and 2 cm wide, often with wavy margins.

FLOWERS: Plants are dioecious. Pollen cones are cylindrical, up to 16 cm long, with a tapered tip. Seed cones are elliptical, up to 20 cm long, with a blunt tip.

FRUITS: Oblong, drupe-like seeds up to 2 cm long, typically brightly colored, some shade of orange.

ROOTS: A large, starchy, tuberous root system that is technically the stem.

DISTRIBUTION AND HABITAT

Distributed from southeast Georgia/Florida to Puerto Rico, occurring in various partially shaded habitats with dry, sandy soils.

FORAGING

The Coontie Palm was a major source of edible starch for the Seminole and Tequesta people. European settlers to southern Florida learned how to extract starch by observing the First People. A major commercial industry developed around starch extraction from Coontie Palm roots, lasting well into the 20th century. The Coontie Palm roots contain water-soluble toxins that would be deadly if not extracted using a combination of water extractions and fermentation. Even the water used to soak the mashed roots can contain lethal toxins. The commercial industry grew, and during WWI, gruel made from starch was the first nourishment gassed soldiers could keep down. The last commercial mill stopped production in 1926 as *Zamia* became increasingly scarce.

QUICK REFERENCE:

USES: edible

FORAGE SEASON(S): spring, summer, fall, winter

FORAGE PART(S): roots

SPECIAL CONCERNS: Some *Zamia* species are endangered. Failure to properly process the *Zamia* root for consumption will leave deadly toxins in the roots that are not fit for human consumption.

QUICK REFERENCE:

USES: edible

FORAGE SEASON(S): late summer through fall

FORAGE PART(S): mushroom

SPECIAL CONCERNS: Do not consume older specimens.

GIANT PUFFBALL

Calvatia gigantea

DESCRIPTION

The Giant Puffball is (true to its name) a large, round, ball-shaped structure on the ground. Individuals are usually about the size of a soccer ball, but there are reports of much larger ones being found (over 1 m across!). The overall shape can be somewhat variable. Typically, they are round, but you can find more irregular or "blob-like" individuals. When young and fresh, they have a soft white color with a velvety texture and a soft, white interior. As the Puffball ages, the outer surface takes on more yellowish or olive tones and becomes smoother, often with inconspicuous scales. The interior of a mature specimen is filled with brownish dust, which is the spores.

DISTRIBUTION AND HABITAT

They can be found throughout North America but are especially common in the eastern half of the United States. They can grow alone or in scattered clusters, in wooded areas, meadow edges, drainage ditches, or under brush, emerging primarily during late summer and fall. At least 15 related species distributed throughout North America generally have a similar appearance but differ in size, coloration, and overall appearance.

FORAGING

The Giant Puffball is a great foraging target for the beginner. They do not have poisonous look-alikes and are easy to identify and find. They should be harvested while white and dense with a firm, spongy interior. Do not harvest soft puffballs that are beginning to turn from white to tannish yellow. At this later stage, they are beginning to produce reproductive spores and are no longer edible. Puffballs can be harvested by simply picking them up off the ground and washing off the soil and debris. A common practice is to cut the Puffball into smaller, bite-size squares. Once harvested, the mushroom should be used immediately or stored in the refrigerator and consumed within a few days. Giant Puffball can be consumed raw but tastes best when prepared with other foods. It has a tofu-like texture and picks up the flavors of the other food used in the recipe.

PHEASANT BACK
DRYAD'S SADDLE

Cerioporus squamosus

DESCRIPTION

This is an annual shelf fungus that is saprobic or parasitic on hardwood trees. They begin growing in spring, often lasting through the year due to their tough and durable composition. It may be found growing solitary or in overlapping clusters on living and dead tree trunks. Occasionally, they are found growing from buried dead wood. The cap can get up to 50 cm across, is 4 cm thick, and is typically kidney or fan-shaped, although they appear more funnel-shaped when growing from buried wood. It is attached to the substrate (what it grows from) via a short, thick stalk. The stalk is mostly white but is eventually covered by a black tomentum (dense wooly, matted hairs). The upper surface of the cap is typically a pale yellow to tan when fresh, with prominent, dark brown scales that are radially arranged. The color tends to fade to more of a whitish color with age. The lower surface of the cap is white or cream-colored and filled with densely packed pores. The pores are barely discernible in young specimens but later become more prominent, with angular openings. The inner flesh is white and soft while young but becomes tough and corky with age.

DISTRIBUTION AND HABITAT

It is widely distributed throughout North America but is most commonly found east of the Great Plains, primarily in deciduous forests. It is known to grow on Maple, Elm, Ash, Willow, and Magnolia.

FORAGING

Pheasant Back mushrooms are one of the earliest mushrooms of the spring and one of the last mushrooms to be seen in the late fall. They are edible but not considered a prime edible for flavor or texture. But what they lack in quality, they make up for in abundance. They grow quickly, and even a novice forager can soon learn to spot and identify the Pheasant Back.

QUICK REFERENCE:

USES: edible
FORAGE SEASON(S): summer, fall
FORAGE PART(S): fruiting body
SPECIAL CONCERNS: none

HEN OF THE WOODS
MAITAKE

Grifola frondosa

DESCRIPTION

Hen of The Woods is a polypore type of mushroom characterized by having dense, cauliflower-like clusters of caps arising from a single, branching stem. The stem grows from an underground sclerotium, a tuber-like structure about the size of a potato. Clusters can grow up to 100 cm wide. Each cap can be up to 10 cm wide, somewhat spoon-shaped, and are a smoky olive, tan, brown, or cream, with noticeable concentric rings of slightly different colors. The underside of the caps is flat, with 1–3 shallow (3 mm) pores per mm. It is said that young specimens give off a pleasant, sweet odor.

DISTRIBUTION AND HABITAT

Grifola frondosa is primarily a denizen of the Eastern hardwood forests of the U.S. and Canada. It is most often found at the base of living Oak trees, on which they are partially parasitic, but may be found on other hardwood species as well. They have also been observed growing from rotting wood. They often reappear in the same spot over several years, typically in late summer/fall.

FORAGING

Hen of the Woods grows on living trees (parasite) and on dead trees (saprophyte) so they are almost always found growing on the hardwood trees they are breaking down. Once you find a Hen of the Woods, you can expect to find another one in the future. The trickiest part about Hen of the Woods forage is cleaning it. Sometimes people are excited to find massive Hen of the Woods mushrooms—but realistically, it is more enjoyable and tastier to find a small, fresh, clean one.

LION'S MANE
MONKEY'S HEAD

Hericium **spp.**

DESCRIPTION

This is a group of fungi that grow on dead or dying wood, with large, white, fleshy fruiting bodies, usually up to 20 cm across. The fruiting bodies may be globular, knob-like, or branched and are covered with many downward-pointing, icicle-like spikes.

DISTRIBUTION AND HABITAT

There are four, possibly five, species of *Hericium* in North America, widely distributed throughout its forested regions, particularly in areas with hardwood species.

FORAGING

Lion's Mane can be found on dead and dying hardwoods, most often observed in the late summer and early fall. It is one of the easiest species for a new forager to identify, and it is easy to clean and prepare. The taste is somewhat like shrimp. It is considered a prime edible to many. It is also reportedly used for medicinal applications, including improved cognitive function, but the research on this has not been conclusive.

QUICK REFERENCE:

USES: edible, medicinal
FORAGE SEASON(S): spring, fall
FORAGE PART(S): fruiting bodies
SPECIAL CONCERNS: none

LOBSTER MUSHROOM

Hypomyces lactifluorum

DESCRIPTION

This is a parasitic fungus that attacks certain species of mushrooms, primarily *Lactarius* and *Russula*. It can quickly overtake its host, enveloping the mushroom in a hard, bright orange covering dotted with small pimples. Over time, the shape of the mushroom is altered into various odd, contorted configurations. Besides modifying its host body, it seemingly can change its flavor for the better, leading to it being a highly sought-after fungus by foragers.

DISTRIBUTION AND HABITAT

Lobsters are widely distributed throughout forested regions of North America.

FORAGING

Lobster Mushrooms typically emerge in late summer, continuing into the fall. They are easy to spot, due to the bright orange color, although once leaves start falling, it becomes more of a challenge. Obviously, they will only be found where their host species are found. In this case, *Lactarius* and *Russula* species form mycorrhizal associations with coniferous and deciduous tree species, especially oaks. Forests containing oak species would be the logical place to start. While you may only find one Lobster in a given forest, more often than not, there will be several widely scattered individuals. When you do find them, remember the spot, because they tend to be found in the same places year after year.

Due to the contorted shapes of Lobsters, a more vigorous cleaning and trimming procedure may be required to remove dirt and other unwanted material. Lobsters have a decent shelf life and may be stored under refrigeration for a couple of weeks. Additionally, they are good candidates for dehydrating, with many aficionados grinding them into a seasoning powder.

QUICK REFERENCE:

USES: edible

FORAGE SEASON(S): late summer and fall

FORAGE PART(S): mushroom

SPECIAL CONCERNS: The Woolly Pine Milk Cap, *Lactarius torminosus*, is toxic (but not deadly) if not cooked and looks like *L. deliciosus*. Some key differences in the Woolly Pine Milk Cap include a hairy cap, white milk, and an association with *Betula* species rather than pines.

DELICIOUS MILK MUSHROOM
SAFFRON MILK CAP
RED PINE MUSHROOM

Lactarius deliciosus

DESCRIPTION

The Delicious Milk Mushroom has a short, hollow stem (<8 cm) and grows up to 2 cm wide. The stem's surface is adorned by many orange-colored scrobiculations (shallow pits). The caps can be up to 20 cm across, initially convex in shape but eventually becoming concave. They are typically some shade of orange, with various amounts of whitish or green mottling. When dry, the cap surface has a granular appearance. When wet, the cap surface becomes sticky. The gills are decurrent (extend down onto the stem), crowded closely together, and are colored orange, turning green when bruised. When the gills are cut or torn, a bright orangish-red latex is exuded, the amount of which is dependent on several factors, including the environmental conditions and age of the mushroom. The latex ultimately turns a wine-red color after exposure to air.

DISTRIBUTION AND HABITAT

The taxonomy of the North American *L. deliciosus*-like species is still being resolved. Likely, *L. deliciosus* is not present in North America but rather a group of several species that all resemble *L. deliciosus*, currently referred to as the *L. deliciosus* group. Members of the *L. deliciosus* group are found in many forested areas of North America, particularly those dominated by pines, but some have been found associated with oak species.

FORAGING

The Delicious Milk Mushroom is considered a "prime edible," and it is a safe beginner mushroom because look-alikes are either edible or not highly toxic. *Lactarius* is a mycorrhizal fungus, and each species tends to form a specific association with a different tree species. Mushrooms in the *Lactarius deliciosus* group tend to be found in conifer forests, typically associated with pines. Look for mushrooms in late summer and fall, often in rings nearby or surrounding pine trees. These can be especially difficult to spot in fall as they blend in with the orange pine needles and leaves on the ground. Once you find one, you will often find several more. These mushrooms should be cooked before consumption. If you are eating a mushroom species for the first time, eat only a small amount to confirm you will not have a poor reaction.

MOREL

Morchella spp.

DESCRIPTION

Morchella are a group of edible fungi that are notable for having caps that have a network of distinctive ridges and pits, giving them a honeycomb-like appearance. Due to their culinary popularity and reluctance to be cultivated, they are one of the most sought-after mushrooms in the wild. Despite their popularity, there is still a lot of taxonomic and eco-logical uncertainty and confusion surrounding this genus. Further adding to the confusion is that as Europeans settled and studied North America, they named many types of fungi, including Morels, after similar-looking species back in their homelands. Modern DNA analysis has shown that in most cases, the North American specimens are not the same species as their doppelgängers across the ocean.

Additionally, temporal and geographic variability within the species led to the naming of many more species than actually exist. Therefore, all the older field guides (and many current ones!) contain incorrect information. Presently, it appears that there are at least 20 species found in North America. They all have a similar appearance: a stereotypical mushroom shape, with a stem bearing a pitted cap-like structure at the tip. They range in height from 2–20 cm, with the caps typically around 4 cm in width. The stems are usually white to pale tan, while the caps can range in color from white to gray to tan to amber to dark brown. The ecological characteristics of the morels are highly variable amongst the species. Some species seem to have mycorrhizal relationships with specific tree species, while others appear to be saprobes. Most species emerge in the spring, but a few emerge later in the year. Some species respond vigorously to fire, producing a "bumper crop" following a burn.

DISTRIBUTION AND HABITAT

As a whole, Morels are widely distributed throughout most of North America. They are most common in areas that are at least moderately forested and are largely absent from non-forested regions, such as the Great Plains and desert Southwest.

FORAGING

Forage for Morels in the early spring, focusing on locations most likely to host Morels. These include wooded areas that have Hickory, Elm, and Ash. Other good spots to scope out include recently burned areas, old sandy flood plains, and abandoned fruit orchards. Morels have a nutty flavor that most mushroom lovers revere.

OYSTER MUSHROOM

Pleurotus spp.

DESCRIPTION

Pleurotus is a genus of saprobic gilled mushrooms that contain some of the most culti-vated and eaten mushrooms in the world. They are typically found growing in clusters on various dead hardwood tree species and have semicircular caps that may be sessile or attached via a rudimentary stalk. Cap size can vary anywhere from 3–20 cm in width. Caps are usually convex in shape when young, becoming flat or concave as they mature. The common name, "Oyster Mushroom," is based on the oyster-shaped cap. Depending on the species, they may be white, gray, yellow, pink, or brownish. The white gills are decurrent, which means they run down the stem. They frequently also have short gills between the longer gills. Spore prints are usually white or pale purple.

DISTRIBUTION AND HABITAT

North America has at least 14 species, widely distributed throughout, wherever their host trees are found.

FORAGING

Oyster Mushrooms can be found from spring to fall. In my region, I often find them in the cooler part of the spring. They are easily identified with their oyster-shaped caps, white, decurrent gills, and presence growing on trees or decaying logs. Once you find a tree that harbors oyster mushrooms, you can expect to be able to forage that spot several times over the mushroom season and for multiple years in a row. Mushrooms should be con-sumed or prepared soon after harvesting. They have a mild, pleasant flavor.

QUICK REFERENCE:

USES: edible
FORAGE SEASON(S): spring, summer, fall
FORAGE PART(S): fruiting bodies
SPECIAL CONCERNS: none

GLOSSARY

ACHENE - The fruit of a plant in the sunflower (*Asteraceae*) family. Fruits are small, hard, and contain one seed.

ADVENTIVE - A non-native plant species that is not widely distributed outside cultivation.

ALKALOID - A class of chemical compounds that are basic and contain at least one nitrogen ring. They tend to have a biological effect on living cells and often have poisonous or medicinal properties.

ALTERNATE - A leaf arrangement where one leaf is attached per node on alternating sides.

ANTHERS - The male reproductive structures on flowering plants. Anthers produce pollen.

BASAL - A leaf arrangement where leaves are arranged on the bottom of the plant.

BIENNIAL - A plant that completes its life cycle over two growing seasons.

BISEXUAL - A flower containing both male and female reproductive structures.

BRACT - A modified leaf that may be showy and adds visual appeal to flowers. The red petals of the Poinsettia are bracts.

CAPSULE - A type of fruit that splits open when ripe, to release the seeds.

CLEISTOGAMOUS - A type of flower that doesn't open, resulting in self-pollination.

CLONAL - A colony of plants that all originate vegetatively from a single individual; thus, all plants in the colony are genetically identical.

COMPOSITE (COMPOSITE TYPE) - The type of flower in the Asteraceae family that is comprised of a dense cluster of tiny flowers (florets) that superficially resemble a single flower. Daisies and sunflowers are examples.

COMPOUND - A type of leaf that is comprised of two or more leaflets that originate from the same petiole.

CONIFER - A type of plant that produces seeds in a cone-like structure called a strobilus and narrow, needle-like leaves. Pines and Spruces are examples.

CORYMBS - A type of flower arrangement in which the uppermost flowers on a stem have the shortest stalks, while the lowermost flowers have the longest stalks, resulting in all of the flowers in the cluster being in the same plane, or flat-topped.

CROSS-SECTION - A cut made at a 90° angle to the central axis of a structure, such as a stem or trunk.

CYME - A type of flower arrangement where the main stem initially produces one terminal flower, followed by a succession of additional flowers produced on lateral branches off the main stem. The terminal flower is the first to open.

DECIDUOUS – Plants, typically trees, that seasonally lose their leaves.

DIMORPHIC – Plants that exhibit two distinct forms of leaves, flowers, or other plant organs, either on the same plant or within plants of the same species.

DIOECIOUS – Plants that produce separate male and female plants.

DISTAL – The part of a structure that is furthest from its point of attachment. For example, the distal part of a leaf would be the tip.

DRUPE – A fruit type distinguished by containing a seed covered by a hard, stony pit surrounded by a fleshy outer layer. Cherries, plums, and almonds are all examples of drupes.

ELLIPTICAL – A leaf shape characterized by having an oval-shaped leaf, wider at the base and tapered near the top. Leaves of this shape are about twice as long as they are wide.

FASCICLE – A cluster of needle-like leaves emerging from the same origin.

FLORET – A small flower that is part of a larger flower arrangement (inflorescence) on a stem.

GLAND (GLANDULAR) – A botanical structure that secretes a substance. They may be internal, or external, either on the plant's outer surface, or at the tip of a hair.

GLOBOSE/GLOBULAR – More or less spherical in shape, as a globe is.

HABIT – A tendency for a plant to have a particular growth form.

HERBACEOUS – A plant that does not produce woody tissues.

HYBRIDIZE – A plant that is the result of the pollination of one plant by another plant that is in a different taxonomic group, whether it be genus, species, variety, etc.

INVOLUCRE – A structure that contains and supports a head, or tight cluster of flowers.

LANCEOLATE – A leaf shape characterized by being about four times longer than wide and tapering to a point at the end.

LATERAL – Referring to something (leaf, branch, etc.) that is attached to the side of another structure.

LAX – Refers to a cluster of something (usually flowers) that are not tightly compact, but rather loose and/or open.

LENTICEL (LENTICULAR) – A type of plant tissue that is porous or loosely packed for purposes of gas exchange. They are often produced on the stems and roots.

LOBE – A part of a structure that is usually a rounded extension of that structure.

MARGIN – The edge of a structure, mostly used when describing leaves.

-MEROUS – A suffix used to describe something that is made up of a certain number of parts, such as four-merous.

MESIC – A condition that is between dry and wet, or moist. Usually used in reference to types of habitats.

MONOECIOUS – A plant that produces separate male and female flowers on the same plant.

NODE – On a plant stem, the region where new leaves, stems, or buds will emerge.

OPPOSITE – A type of leaf arrangement where two leaves are attached per node and are arranged opposite each other along the stem.

OVARY – The female reproductive organ of a flowering plant. After fertilization of a flowering plant, the ovary will develop into the fruit.

PALMATE – A leaf with midribs that radiate outwards from a central point in a palm-like fashion.

PANICLE – An inflorescence type characterized by flowers loosely arranged in a spike with many branches.

PEDICEL – A stalk that attaches the flower to the stem.

PERENNIAL – A plant that persists for multiple growing seasons.

PERFECT – A flower that includes all male and female reproductive structures.

PERFOLIATE – A leaf with the base wrapped entirely around the stem.

PETIOLE – The stem-like attachment between a stem and the leaf.

PHYTOCHEMICAL – A chemical produced by a plant; often these are compounds that have unique properties that support the plant's ability to defend against pathogens and pests.

PINNATE – A leaf that is subdivided into leaflets. Leaves can have multiple levels of such division.

POD – A fruit type characterized by being dry at maturity and dehiscent (splitting) along both sides to release seeds. Peas and beans produce pods.

POME – A fruit type characterized by having a fleshy layer surrounding a core. An apple is a pome.

PROPAGULE – Any non-sexual reproductive structure in plants (bulbils, rhizomes, tubers, etc.)

RACEME – An inflorescence characterized by having flowers arranged on the main stalk, attached on short stalks, and equidistant from each other along the main stem.

RESIN – A substance produced by plants that is thick, sticky, and either translucent or clear. Amber (fossilized resin), frankincense, and hashish are examples.

RHIZOME (RHIZOMATOUS GROWTH) – A horizontal, underground stem often used for plant vegetative reproduction.

ROSETTE – An arrangement of leaves growing in a rose-like cluster, usually at the base of the plant.

SEPAL – The outer whorl of leaf-like or petal-like structures on a flower. Sepals typically surround the flower when it is in the bud.

SESSILE – Describing a leaf attached to the stem with no petiole.

SIMPLE – Describing a leaf shape that is not further divided or lobed.

STAMEN – The male reproductive structures of the flower, including the anthers that produce pollen.

STIGMA – The portion of the female reproductive structures on a flower that is receptive to pollen.

STOLON (STOLONIFEROUS) – Horizontal plant stems growing above ground.

STYLE – A stalk that connects a plant's stigma and ovary.

SUCKERING – Vertical vegetative outgrowths of new plant shoots.

TAPROOT – A large, main root of a dicot plant.

TEPAL – A floral structure that is either a petal or a sepal but has a similar appearance. Tepals are often observed in lily flowers where the outermost whorl of the flower is made of sepals that appear petal-like.

TERMINAL – Usually referring to the buds or growth at the very tips of the stem.

TUBER – A plant's underground, vegetative reproductive structure. Of a starch storage organ.

UNISEXUAL – A plant that is either male or female.

UNLOBED – A leaf that does not have lobes or is not further subdivided with lobes.

UTRICLE – A small, sac-like structure on a plant.

WHORL – The arrangement of plant parts (usually floral structures) that radiate from a central point.

AUTHOR BIOS

DR. KIT CARLSON earned her PhD in plant microbiology and pathology at the University of Missouri, and conducted her postdoctoral research at Virginia Tech, focused on molecular diagnostics of plant disease. Kit has been a botany professor for nearly two decades. During her tenure, she has served thousands of students and developed and instructed more than 15 different plant science courses. She and her students have conducted and published research on a wide range of topics, including plant disease, medicinal plants, ethnobotany, public land, science education, and more. She is also the author of *The Book of Killer Plants*.

AARON CARLSON is an award-winning naturalist recognized for his contributions to observing rare plant species in their native habitats. Aaron received his BS in Biology and Wildlife at the University of Wisconsin-Stevens Point, and attended the University of Missouri for his graduate work in limnology. When not working as an educator or lab technician, Aaron spends his free time observing and documenting the life histories of lichens, plants, fungi, and animals. Aaron lives in southern Wisconsin with his wife, two children, and their poodle.

INDEX

ABOUT CIDER MILL PRESS BOOK PUBLISHERS

Good ideas ripen with time. From seed to harvest, Cider Mill Press brings fine reading, information, and entertainment together between the covers of its creatively crafted books. Our Cider Mill bears fruit twice a year, publishing a new crop of titles each spring and fall.

VISIT US ON THE WEB AT

cidermillpress.com

OR WRITE TO US AT

501 Nelson Place
Nashville, TN 37214